# Stop Overthinking

>>>———————————<<<

The Complete guide
to
declutter your mind,
ease anxiety, and turn
off your intensive
thoughts.
Overcome indecision
and procrastination for
a stress-Free Life. For
men and
women.

>>>———————————<<<

written by Sebasti

To whom is trying to find a way to take the driver seat of their life.

Good luck.

# table of contents

Introduction     01

Chapter 1     06
What exactly is overthinking?

Chapter 2     21
How to focus on your present

Chapter 3     35
How to get rid of mental junk

Chapter 4     47
I'm not my thoughts, I'm what I do

Chapter 5     58
Perfectionism vs excellence

Chapter 6     71
Indecisiveness and how to fight it

Chapter 7     86
Procrastination cure

Chapter 8     100
Mindfulness meditation

Conclusions     113

# Introduction

Do you ever feel like you overthink every single thing? So much so that it has become an obsession - clouding your judgment and preventing you from doing what you want in life - taking risks or reaching your potential?

Since you picked up this book, I would assume that you are no stranger to lying awake at night ruminating over the happenings of that day - or even something you did months or years ago. Your mind may be weighed down with regrets, "what-if" s, or niggling worries that actually blur your vision from seeing whatever is right in front of you. As a result, you are living in the past or future, and missing the most precious gift of all - the present.

You are not alone. As humans, we are all profound and reflective thinkers - and of course, this isn't a bad thing! Quite the contrary - this is what has allowed our species to progress thus far - it has been our ticket to civilization - to inventions, to progress, to modern life as we know it. This ability to think beyond the here and now, to reflect, to plan, to self-criticize.

However, thanks to this evolutionary quirk that just so happened to nudge our species into the stone age and beyond, today, many of us get into the habit of thinking every tiny detail and ruminating over every risk or setback. So much so, that we struggle to enjoy our lives, or dare to dive into the future that we want.

Not to mention that overthinking can even lead to anxiety and depression if not taken care of, as it can seriously hinder our mental clarity and emotional wellbeing.

But how do you know if you're an overthinker?

Here are 8 tell-tale signs:

1. You replay embarrassing moments in your head over and again...

2. You have trouble sleeping because it feels like your brain won't slow down or switch off.

3. You are often asking yourself "what if"... "What if I had chosen the other option?" "What if I fail?" "What if I'm not good enough?"

4. You spend a lot of time thinking about the potential hidden meanings behind things – "Is she not replying because of something I said?" "When I said that, did he think I was stupid?" "Were they looking at me like that because they were talking about me?"

5. You ruminate over previous conversations you had with people, and think about all the things you could have or should have said.

6. You constantly relive mistakes, criticism, or moments that bring back negative feelings in your head.

7. You are sometimes not fully aware of what's going on around you because you're too busy obsessing over what happened in the past, or what may happen in the future.

8. You spend a lot of time worrying about things outside of your control.

Does any of this sound familiar? If so, then stay with me!

The research is pretty clear — overthinking can be harmful both for mental and physical health (not to mention life satisfaction and success!) and actually doesn't help to prevent or solve your problems. Psychological research on the subject has revealed the following concerning statistics:

- Thanks to modern living, 73% of 25–35-year-olds, 52% of 45–55-year-olds and 20% of 65–75-year-olds are chronic overthinkers.
- Overthinking contributes to severe depression and anxiety and interferes with problem-solving abilities.
- Overthinking significantly increases the risk of unhealthy eating and drinking habits, and other self-harming behaviors, including smoking and drug abuse.

But fear not - you can learn to let go of this harmful habit. To loosen up a bit, and remember how to have fun. How to sleep at

night without obsessively thinking about every "what if" your mind haunts you with. How to make a choice with confidence and feel excited and positive when you think about your future, rather than full of doubt.

The secret? You need to reset your approach to life. To learn how to be okay with not being perfect, with making mistakes, and with not always knowing exactly where the future will lead. Scrap that - to not only "be okay" with all of these things, but to realize that this is what keeps life interesting - and above all, a learning and self-development experience. Many of us think we want perfection and predictability - but this would get boring pretty quickly if we had our way!

And so, through some lessons, examples, and tips - I invite you to delve into some of the latest psychological research and tactics when it comes to this ever-increasing global disease that is overthinking - and remember how to switch off from time to time, to ensure we don't burn our poor overworked brains out.

Whether you're a workaholic, a perfectionist parent or partner, or tend to obsess about your productivity and set very high standards for yourself, setting your head into a constant spin - then this book may be just what you need. We are all overthinkers at times, but the sooner you learn some coping mechanisms to not let obsessive worrying or racing thoughts disrupt your life or goals - the better.

To briefly introduce myself and my background, my name is Sebastian O'Brien. I was born in Ireland, 1980 and have worked as a Psychotherapist and counselor for many years. I support a whole range of individuals who are struggling with overthinking and anxiety - both through my face-to-face consultations and now, much to my excitement, via my book! This has always been a dream of mine - to be able to reach countless more individuals who are grappling with these all-too-common mental hurdles, by sharing my years of experience and research in an accessible way through the pages you hold before you.

Here's the thing: the link between overthinking and mental health complications is a chicken-and-egg type of situation. Overthinking is linked to psychological problems, like depression and anxiety - but do we overthink because we are anxious and depressed, or are we anxious and depressed because we overthink? Most likely, it actually goes both ways. And this is why this is such a toxic vicious cycle. Once you are in it, it's hard to break out. Many spend years or even decades on a perpetually spinning hamster wheel of thinking, and anxiety, and more thinking, and more anxiety...

On top of that, "analysis paralysis" is a real problem. This means that the more options you feel you have before you, the more you think. And the more you think, the more trapped you feel. So much choice that you feel that the choice is actually taken away from you. Yes, French philosophers have been talking about this for some time now, but in this increasingly materialistic and overwhelming world, it is more relevant than ever this overwhelmed feeling many of us get as a symptom of a modern (and often pretty successful) life.

We all have plenty on our plate - this is a fact of life. I am, of course, not claiming that I can fix all the problems on your mind. However, what I can do is teach you how to better approach your problems, so that they become less of an emotional burden. This, in turn, will allow you to be better able to fix them or manage them for yourself.

If you overcome the urge to ruminate and overthink every single worry or "what-if" in your life - you will be able to overcome your self-destructive and self-punishing mental habits for yourself, to make you better equipped and more emotionally resilient to handle the inevitable turbulence that will come your way. This, I can promise you.

Ultimately, I will show you how to tap into a new realm of inner peace and mental clarity to transform the way you problem-solve and approach your life's challenges. Live in the moment, and you won't waste it obsessing over past mistakes or future threats.

Learning how to think clearly and give your mind the rest and space it needs could be your ticket to mental wellness and contentment.

# Chapter 1

## What exactly is overthinking?

The Ancient Greek stoic thinker, Socrates was perhaps onto something when he proclaimed:

'the unexamined life is not worth living.'

However, I would add that the overly examined life isn't one I would personally recommend either. As with most things in life, it's all about balance.

And then there's Descartes' 'I think therefore I am,' mantra - that didn't catch on as much as it did for nothing!

Thinking is - though I don't mean to claim this ground-breaking idea as my own - pretty darn useful. And by calling out overthinking, I do not by any means wish to discourage deep thinking in itself. Rather, as with any addictive and self-destructive behavior, overthinking is harmful. It takes what are perhaps the most valuable abilities we possess as a species - critical thinking and imagination - and turns them up to 100, burning out our minds and our emotional capacity along with it.

In fact, if you have a tendency to overthink, it can be completely ravaging to both your mental and physical processes. It sends the brain's stress response into overdrive, inducing the fight-or-flight response. As a result, your brain and body are flooded with the stress hormones cortisol and adrenaline - and not only during those sporadic and brief periods where danger is imminent, as this response is designed for, but any time your thoughts start to wander into overthinking territory…

In this sense, you could say that Humanity actually evolved to become a species of overthinkers. Despite our cognitive ability putting us literally a head and shoulders above the Animal

Kingdom, we still have the same primitive fight or flight mechanism, but now whipped up into a toxic cocktail with our human love of THINKING. Essentially, we are now doomed to 'think ourselves into stress.' Thanks to our ruminating brains - no threat is ever truly gone! The things you lie awake thinking about at night - are any of them an immediate threat to your life? Does thinking about them incessantly ever solve anything?

Since our nervous systems haven't been able to keep up with our newfound thinking abilities - they continue to flood our bodies with the hormones to keep us alert and panicked enough to spring out of harm's way - and so we stay perpetually alert… and perpetually ready to run. Is it any wonder we can't switch off? Or that anxiety, insomnia, and panic disorders are becoming increasingly widespread in the modern world?

We end up physically and emotionally exhausted, oscillating between jittery anxiety and overwhelming, apathetic fatigue, once our body's overused adrenaline supply eventually dries up.

## Overthinking explained

*Is overthinking a disorder? Why is it bad?*

So, to start right at the beginning. What is overthinking? Why does it happen? And what's the difference between rumination, introspection, problem-solving, and self-reflection? I must first clarify that in most cases, although not ideal, overthinking it is not necessarily pathological or cause for medication, and you can work on overcoming it - all you need is the right techniques and advice. However, it does require a thorough understanding of the thought mechanisms, the neurophysiological response, and the triggers - so that you are aware of what overthinking looks like, why you do it, and most importantly - how to stop it in its tracks!

As mentioned, overthinking isn't a disorder or an illness in itself. Rather, it's a trap we all fall into from time to time. And although this means no one is exempt, on a more positive note, it also means no one is cursed with it forever! However, overthinking is still a potentially harmful and self-sabotaging habit that should be taken very seriously, as when an individual can't stop obsessing and irrationally worrying over things in the long term, and regardless of circumstances (in other words, it's not a temporary state due to a particular life event or a temporary concern), it can interfere severely with their mental health and quality of life.

All in all, overthinking is as common as breathing in this modern world of both endless possibility and endless stress. The worries of the world are just one click or swipe away, and our sphere of concern is stretched far beyond its natural limitations - biologically intended only for a select few in your family or tribe. In today's reality of globalization and digital connectivity, we are exposed both to more information and more trauma - and this doesn't go unnoticed by our subconscious. It's a great thing to be able to communicate and receive news from all four corners of the world, but our poor minds are not wired to expand our empathy to such a degree. Therefore, we are not mentally prepared to process so much emotional stimulation and cope with such a fast-paced world. Is it any wonder, then, that our minds tend to spiral out of control if we don't make the required effort to keep ourselves grounded?

Many clients also have complaints of reliving past failures, mistakes, or traumas over and over again; they feel simply unable to move past them, forgive themselves or heal and move on. Many also struggle to stop their relentless worrying about their goals and future tasks - until they feel almost impossible to accomplish. And for others, it's the obsession with what others think of them that keeps them up at night. Did I offend them? did I embarrass myself? What must they think of me? And so on.

So, which one is your poison?

Overall, the obstacle to vanquish is this (perceived) inability to slow down the racing of thoughts, worries or emotions - that only incites a vicious cycle of anxiety and chronic stress. Whatever your demons are, you must work on not allowing them to torment you. I hope to not inspire any further anxiety in you when I say that this will only lead to further mistakes or general unease. In this way, you are not permitting yourself to be calm: to simply experience the present moment (more on that later!) and allow the natural rhythms of your thoughts to flow with ease - unshaken by your intrusive spiraling.

# "I'm just problem solving"
*The difference between overthinking and problem-solving.*

You may be one of those overthinkers that claims it's all just necessary problem-solving. "I can't pretend my problems don't exist," or "someone has to think about these things," may be mantras of yours when having to explain your deep thoughts - either to others or just to yourself. However, it's an easy mistake to make to confuse overthinking with innocent problem-solving. You might convince yourself that letting your worries spin around your mind in this way is productive. However, don't forget that the solution to a problem doesn't tend to come more easily simply by *thinking harder*. In fact, some of our greatest emotional clarity comes from adequate physical and emotional rest and distancing one's worries.

On the topic of overthinking versus problem-solving, Michael D. Yapko, a clinical psychologist in Fallbrook, California, states that 'most people who engage in rumination don't know they're ruminating; they think they're problem-solving – not being able to distinguish between the two is part of the problem. If it doesn't lead to a timely and effective course of specific action, it's rumination.'

Think of it this way: a simple definition of problem-solving is actively looking for the solution to an issue. You will know if you are problem-solving when you notice a decrease in stress as you work on untangling the mess of thoughts you were presented with. On the other hand, overthinking involves over-analysis and rumination (which I will come to next!). This only spurs you to dwell on your worries and prevents you from having the mental capacity to coin a solution for yourself. Overthinking magnifies every minute issue, or even unlikely possibilities - making you focus on the worst-case scenarios as though they are already set in stone.

Indeed, the human mind is cruel like that; the more you think, the more darkness you create for yourself—causing you to be stuck in a state of perpetual anxiety.

## The different types of deep thinking
*What are rumination, self-reflection, and introspection?*

Time for some key terms: rumination, self-reflection, and introspection: but what do these all mean? There is an important difference between rumination - something to be avoided - and the other two - which are to be aimed for. Not all deep thoughts are equal! Of course, with the promise of personal growth and increased creativity, time spent alone to ponder the complexities of your own life can be a positive and productive experience. This opportunity to mull things over can be hugely beneficial to your emotional state and mental clarity, and your saving grace if you are feeling overwhelmed or uncertain. You have a bafflingly complex and powerful brain - so use it! But use it wisely. However, if we are negatively turned against ourselves or become obsessive or compulsive in our thought-processes, then this time spent in reverie can also become dangerous. So how can we be sure what kind of thinking we are engaging in - to make sure that it is not harming us, but nourishing us?

## Rumination

Let's begin with rumination - the one to be avoided, being one of the modern human's greatest downfalls. Technically, rumination is simply the technical term for "overthinking," occurring when you become trapped in a negative cycle of circular thinking that can trigger episodes of depression or paranoia. As put by Steve Ilardi, associate professor of Clinical Psychology at the University of Kansas: "rumination involves dwelling repetitively and at length on negative thoughts, often related to failure, rejection, humiliation, loss or retaliation."

I also get behind fellow psychologist Susan Nolen-Hoeksema's definition of rumination as "...repeatedly and passively thinking about the causes or consequences of problems without moving to active problem-solving." For example, ruminating about your weight instead of taking action to change it for the better. Ruminating about what someone thinks of you instead of engaging with them to correct any potential misunderstanding. Or, ruminating about how much you despise your job and yet doing nothing to change your situation. Sound familiar?

The thing is, every person is divided between a healthy attitude toward themselves - you know, that goal-directed and life-affirming voice that takes over sometimes, when you're feeling your best, keeping your head above water, your worries at bay, and your eyes on the prize? But then there's the self-destructive side that we all must also manage. That critical, paranoid, and suspicious voice that lures you away from your goals and squashes your self-esteem every chance it gets. Making you believe you shouldn't or you can't. That people think badly of you or that you are a failure. This inner critic can take over our thinking if we don't manage to get a hold over it, which is what leads to rumination.

However, when this less desirable side of our consciousness is kept in check, we are capable of having a more positive and self-reflection, realistic and yet untarnished by our negative thoughts.

The trap is that in-depth thought DOES often lead to useful and necessary insights. In a sense, by thinking deeply about our life and how we go about navigating it, we are walking on a knife's edge - one slip and we tumble into the hard-to-escape depths of rumination. Just as with anything, if you get used to reaping positive results, you will repeat the activity. This is called the habit loop, and I discussed it at length in my previous book, Self-Confidence Training. These behaviors then become associated with benefits and lodged into our mind as go-to activities. As such, they tend to be very tricky to change.

But rumination won't get you anywhere - as it's like getting stuck. Your wheels are spinning furiously, but you just won't budge...

## Self-Reflection

So what can we turn to instead of rumination during those quiet moments where we really have a chance to consider how we are living our lives? Enter: self-reflection.

Essentially, self-reflection is exactly what it implies - an ability to reflect upon yourself in a clear-headed and objective way. When you engage in true self-reflection, you really see yourself: your actions, the way you behave and interact with others, and how you could work on your current attributes. Self-reflection means seeing yourself for who you are.

This may sound simple - of course you can see yourself, right? Don't we all already know "who we are"? Well, I assure you that most people really don't. We may know what our reflection looks like in the mirror. We may know our first name, our surname, heck - we know our mother's maiden name and the time and date that we were born. You know your qualifications and you know (at least, I hope!) how to do your job. But do you know what lies beneath all of that? When you take away what anyone can find on your birth certificate, passport, resume, or social media page - what is left? Because there is, of course, more to you than all of that... but what?

Don't worry - the mere realization of this is the first big step towards a more positive way of processing your thoughts.

## Introspection

At this stage, it's time to take our self-reflection even further. To not only look at ourselves in this way, but to then go on to delve deeper behind the surface and carry out a more thorough self-analysis. This is where introspection comes in.

Introspection is the process of healthy self-examination and self-discovery, which is a crucial first step when it comes to establishing healthier mental and emotional habits. Essentially, introspection is the act of "checking in" with yourself as you would a dear friend - to see where you're at emotionally. When you take this valuable time to be introspective, we must adopt a curious, open-minded, accepting, and self-compassionate attitude. Then think about what you would like to challenge in yourself, and how you want to distance yourself from negative influences - either from your current situation, or from your past. In this way, you will be able to give your life and goals more meaning and more intentional direction, yet without falling victim to your inner-critic - which only serves to hold you back.

You may feel as though you are exploring something; considering new perspectives and deeper meanings behind your thoughts, feelings, and actions. You feel like you have a direction, a purpose, and are heading directly to the answers and awareness you seek. Conversely, rumination feels like going round in circles, and sinking deeper into distress. And so, to avoid tipping over into rumination territory, I strongly encourage people to develop self-compassion and self-awareness. Compassion so that you can be more encouraging and forgiving to yourself and keep your thoughts constructive and forward-thinking, and awareness so that you can recognize for yourself when your thoughts are becoming self-sabotaging, and so you can pull yourself out of rumination's grip when need be.

In essence, introspection is the "next one up" of self-reflection, if you will. It involves not only the observation of the self, but also the examination of one's own mental and emotional state of mind. As such, introspection is a deeply personal and even philosophical act of self-analysis, where you analyze your thoughts, behaviors and beliefs for what they are - a reflection of the experiences that formed you since birth.

## When overthinking becomes dangerous for your mental health

*Could this habit stem from your childhood?*

Some mental health diagnoses have overthinking as a key element - such as post-traumatic stress disorder (PTSD), panic disorder, various anxiety disorders, or severe phobias. However, for the vast majority of us, overthinking is simply a part of life - not an indication of an illness - and something we can manage all on our own once we discover how. That being said, overthinking is still harmful - even for the healthiest of minds.

A recent study found that when people overthink after a stressful experience, since they don't give their already-exhausted mind a break after the trauma, forcing it to replay the turmoil over and over, it takes them longer to recover emotionally. On the other hand, by using constructive tactics such as distraction or mindfulness meditation, individuals were shown to psychologically heal a lot better from their past struggles.

Other research revealed that people with a higher tendency to overthink experience "exaggerated and prolonged increases in their blood pressure and heart rate in response to mental stress." This is hugely concerning and can contribute to long-term blood pressure and, thus, a greater risk of cardiovascular complications over time.

And as a secondary consequence of overthinking, there are various harmful behaviors we feel more inclined to engage in as a consequence of our body's reaction to stress. For instance, overeating high-sugar and high-fat foods in order to replicate the serotonin ("happy hormone") our worn out brains are lacking - or to satisfy our survival instinct's cravings for high-calorie sustenance as it believes you are in an emergency situation where food may be scarce.

Then there's the overconsumption of alcohol, smoking, or the use of recreational drugs - all of which don't need too much explaining, as it's common knowledge how we can all-too-easily become dependent on any drug that offers our anxious minds some respite - no matter how damaging they are do the rest of our bodies. This just illustrates how much stress and overthinking really gets to us! We literally sacrifice our physical health in order to try and feel some temporary peace.

Finally, there are the health consequences such as an increased risk of depression, anxiety, and insomnia - all of which you are at a much higher risk of if you are an overthinker, and which can change your entire outlook on life for the worse. This, of course, can also lead to further health problems down the road.

So no, it's not all in your head. Overthinking can actually negatively impact every part of your body.

## The Gender Bias

Here's an interesting element to the overthinking conversation I simply couldn't leave out - how your gender may affect your rumination and stress tendencies.

Although, stereotypically, - women have an easier time with introspection and self-reflection than men - being considered the more emotionally attuned of the sexes as a general rule (which could be thanks to their psychological hardwiring as the nurturers and empathises of the species) - whether related or not, they also have a harder time with rumination.

This isn't to say that all women are ruminators, or are more so than their male peers - but it is a fact that if you're a woman, you're at a higher risk of becoming a chronic overthinker… And according to recent scientific research, women are shown to ruminate more often than men do. Maybe there's some truth behind the age-old stereotype that women hone in on the details, whereas men tend to focus on the overall picture?

Other research suggests that women and men have tendencies to ruminate about different things. For instance, men are reported to overthink about work and finances. On the other hand, women are more sensitive to conflict and the illness or death of loved ones as their rumination triggers. Again, this research is both controversial and interesting. It sheds light on how our biology and sociology can impact what we prioritize and fear most in life.

It begs the question: is it the tendency to ruminate itself that women are more prone to, or simply the more social and relationship-focused priorities of most women that can more easily take them down rumination road?

Some psychologists propose that these disparities are rooted in different social statuses, life conditions, and inequalities that still take hold of our societies. For instance, the subconscious beliefs that we are conditioned with from childhood that men should be financially successful providers, and women should be nurturing, and live for their bonds with others. But I'm not here to argue whether these societal norms are right, wrong, natural, or completely made up - I'm just here to tell you that they exist - whether or not you personally subscribe to them! And so, even the most forward-thinking men and women can fall prey to these gendered insecurities, and our data on rumination is shaped as a result.

Of course, all of this could either be a result of nature, nurture, or most likely - a combination of the two. From our hormone profiles to our upbringings and how our gender is expected to behave - there are myriad factors whenever a gender discrepancy like this one emerges. All you need to know is that anyone can succumb to rumination - in fact, to some extent, we all do. The key is how you acknowledge and then learn to manage it.

## "Tell me about your childhood…"

Similarly, a study in Psychiatry Research found that people who experienced early life stress - such as emotional or sexual abuse or trauma - have an increased likelihood of being more of an overthinker as an adult. It's simply our frazzled mind's attempt to piece things together and make sense of things. But of course, it doesn't always do this successfully. And naturally, early exposure to the bad side of humanity is likely to shape your outlook throughout your life.

If you experienced intense stress early on in life, even before your brain had the chance to fully mature, then this "frazzled" state is even more severe, and so your brain is whirring away, desperately trying to make sense of the senseless in a tragically obsolete exercise.

## How to Problem-Solve Without Ruminating

So whatever your gender, social status, or childhood - what can you do to stop overthinking and rumination in its tracks, while still remaining focused on our self-development and self-aware of where we may be able to improve?

Well, instead of replaying past experiences in your mind's eye, make a plan. What can you do to take action about that situation you can't stop thinking about? There's always something - even if it takes some thinking to get there. Perhaps confronting the person who you had a conflict with? Investing in training to make sure you are better prepared for whatever looming tasks is making you shudder? Letting your boss know that you're overworked and setting down some boundaries?

Whatever you decide, you must do to improve your current anguish, write it out as your action plan. Even if you're not ready to take it, simply seeing it in black and white will start the ball rolling.

The mind behind the Huffington Post and Thrive Global, Arianna Huffington, advises setting a particular time for rumination, or "worry time" as she calls it. Perhaps, for example, between 6:00-6:10 pm, after returning from work, but before preparing dinner, you set aside some time to simply THINK. Think about whatever is on your mind, threatening your inner-peace. Think it to death. But then, when the time's up, resume your other activities. You have given these worries their fair share of your attention, and have hopefully gotten your urge to ruminate out of your system. Any more time would be a waste and could lead to spiraling. And so, between these established "worry time" appointments, refuse to give into your rumination: you're too busy doing something else much more worthwhile!

There is a theory that people often "just know" whether their deep thoughts are damaging or productive. You may know that it's the former and continue anyway, but be honest - you know. There is a different feeling that comes along with each one: if you're ruminating, you almost feel guilty about it - like you're indulging in a naughty habit, and yet all it brings you is pain. Yet set out to think things through rationally and strategically, and it seems like something to be proud of. You feel lighter; more full of energy and motivation than you did before - even if no huge revelation comes from it. You simply know in your gut that you're on the right track.

So how do you distinguish whether you're in a pessimistic overthinking mode, or realistic problem-solving - to prepare for future obstacles?

Whether you're ruminating over a workplace matter, or stressing yourself out over a family issue, the key is to ask yourself whether there is any method or strategy behind those racing thoughts. Are you genuinely making an effort to piece together the components of your dilemma in a clear-headed and solution-oriented way, or simply allowing your panic to take over and scramble your perspective even further, only increasing your anguish over the situation?

Make your thinking more productive and less destructive by being aware of when you are investing more time than necessary or mentally healthy - thinking about a particular situation on your mind. If you're problem-solving - in other words, calmly and strategically mulling over the issue with your focus set on how to solve and move past it - then, by all means, keep going. However, if it turns out you are overthinking - chewing over the issue mercilessly but refusing to swallow it and move on - then make an active decision to refuse to waste any more time or mental energy. Cast it out of your mind, at least for now, either by focusing on a more productive task or thought - or, as I will delve into more later on, by practicing mindfulness meditation.

Once you figure out how to swap your overthinking for genuine problem-solving, you can then channel your time and mental energy into productive activities. You'll gather the emotional strength to devote yourself to fixing rather than ruminating over your worries, which will ultimately help you reach your full, uninhibited potential.

# Redeem your bonus!

Hi!

Sorry for the interruption, I truly hope that you are enjoying the book.

I just wanted to tell you that purchasing "Stop overthinking" you have access to my pdf training on Self-confidence.

This training is the base of my first book about how to face your fears and build unshakable self-esteem.

Why am I sharing this with you? Because I truly want to give you a great value with this book, and I reckon self-confidence and overthinking are strictly related.

Back to these worksheets, they are packed in a in pdf so you can download and print them! It will allow you to keep track of your improvements and if you need to redo them in the future.

Download your PDF!

In addition, I will send you some interesting facts and myths about self-confidence and overthinking by e-mail, don't let go away this opportunity!

Well, thank you for your time and now let's pick up where we left off!

# Chapter 2

## How to focus on your present

Now it's time to refocus. If you really think about it, it becomes clear that most of our overthinking woes boil down to constantly jumping to the past and future. What happened, what could have happened, what might happen... Most of us don't sit there ruminating over what's right before our eyes - the color of the wall or whatever you can see out of the window. No - overthinking is a time-traveling activity. It causes us to look backward, forwards - anywhere but the present moment.

Even if the idea of focusing on the present may seem basic or obvious, it can really make a profound difference to your chronic overthinking habit. This is because living life in the present is essential for our wellbeing. However, we are wired to think continuously, both about the past - which risks triggering depression, self-resentment, and a lack of self-confidence - or to the future - which often sparks the fear of failure, performance anxiety, and unrealistic expectations.

Life must be lived in the present moment so that we are able to fully enjoy our mental and physical energies in the present and get rid of the weight of overthinking.

Although a bit of a pain at times, this ability to "time travel" with our thoughts is what makes us human. However pensive your cat may look or however quizzical your dog seems as they stare into space - scientists reiterate that it is most likely only humans - with the possible exception of some great apes and sea mammals - who are donned with this cognitive capacity to think about past events, or ponder the future. A cat most likely is thinking about that bird in the sky. A dog is most often thinking about the fun or food they are or are not having. Humans, on the other hand, lose this primitive stream of consciousness shortly after infancy.

If we clutter our brains, and thus our lives, with painful memories, feelings, and worries, there's little room for anything more positive. To improve your state of mind, you must realize that it's your choice whether to hold onto resentment, bitterness, or even fear. Although we often can't choose whether we experience these feelings as they inevitably come and go, gripping onto them as many of us do, is entirely our decision - even if we often don't see it that way.

## Humans: The Mental Time-Travellers

You could say overthinking is part of the human condition, and I would agree with this sentiment to a certain extent - as I believe it is a part of the modern human condition. Let me explain: as touched upon in the first chapter, the human body's issue with stress is linked to our ancient stress response - which evolved not only when we had a whole different lifestyle containing threats far-removed from office politics, mortgage worries, and marital quarrels - but let's not forget that we had a more primitive brain.

Back then, our ancestors were led primarily by the hippocampus - but now our brains have evolved to have a prefrontal cortex too. What does that mean? Well, it means that we now have the ability to look to the past and to the future - as well as think about whatever happens to be in a periphery at a given time. To consider alternative decisions to take, fabricate alternative scenarios in our head, and contemplate our own existence and identity.

And thanks to this curious combination of biology and sociology, we all overthink things at times. We are wired to flee imminent dangers like an animal is, but also to contemplate more abstract concepts, which makes us human. You may be overly concerned with what you said or did to somebody. Did you offend them? Do they hate you now? Alternatively, you may be worried about your performance at school or at work. Or perhaps about your personal relationships. These things would not even be comprehensible to a primitive human - let alone cause for anxiety!

Worse still: today, many of us aren't only often anxious, but we then go on to develop meta-anxiety - that is, anxiety about being anxious. It all starts with worrying about what will happen in the future, which then often takes you down a rumination road of what happened in the past and how things could have been different. Have you noticed what's missing?

Sure, we often get anxious about what is happening in the present moment too, but unless we are under some sort of attack or facing an imminent threat, this is connected to worry of a different time period. We may worry about a look someone gives us or a comment someone makes in the present - but only because of what this may mean in the future. Humans are funny in that way - we just can't seem to stay in the present moment. We expend so much time and energy obsessing over what has or will happen, that we actually lose sight of what is happening right now.

There are also those "what if" scenarios, where you consider what could happen in a variety of circumstances, often paired with an irrational bout of catastrophizing - that is, thinking the worst will happen and letting your imagination run wild with these possibilities. Intrusive or obsessive thoughts are also a common experience. This is where - no matter how much you try to shut down upsetting thoughts or distract yourself from your incessant worries, they keep rearing their ugly heads to monopolize your every waking thought process.

# Forgiving the past

*Learning from mistakes and practising self-forgiveness.*

And so, as humans, we are perhaps doomed to overthink our past and future in this way. After all, the ability to do so has gotten us far! That being said, we need to learn how to turn off this ability so as not to spiral into rumination territory and burn ourselves out. After all, whatever happens in our past - good or (perhaps especially) bad - has the potential to teach us valuable lessons about how to improve our present and future. And so, rather than dwelling on past mistakes or traumas, it is both the self-compassionate and the constructive thing to do to forgive yourself and use this insight for personal growth and self-improvement.

Say, for example, you have two dogs, but one day, one of them passes away. You may spend days, or even weeks, mourning the lost dog. Thinking about how you could have appreciated her more, showed her even more love, somehow done more for her. Then one day, you realize that you don't want to have those feelings again the day the other day dies. Rather than focusing on the dog that you lost, your perception shifts as you suddenly realized you are still blessed with the dog you have. Instead of wallowing over your loss, you channel your mental energy into loving and caring for the other. In this way, you not only distract yourself from rumination over "what ifs," but you also ensure that you learn from any mistakes you made previously and do what you can to avoid similar regrets in the future.

It doesn't matter whether you have or even like dogs - I guarantee there will be some sort of parallel in your life -where you have focused so much on what you don't have, that you forget to enjoy what you do have. Often, the best way to "forgive" or accept the past is to allow the lessons you learned to take shape in your present.

Why do we hold on to the past, specifically? Why is it so easy to ruminate over experiences that only inflict pain, embarrassment, or regret whenever we do? As you will probably know all too well, those who hold onto their past negative experiences often relive the pain they felt back then over and over in their tormented minds. So how can we stop this mental self-harm? How can we get out of our heads and move on?

The only way you can let more positivity into your mind is to make space for it. To lose some baggage, and open yourself up to more positive thoughts and ideas. However, things don't tend to just disappear all on their own. You need to make the commitment for yourself and stick to it. Making a conscious decision to simply "let go" in this way also means accepting that you actually have a choice to let it go - which is an uplifting and empowering revelation itself, that has the potential to change your life in the longer term.

## Past = Familiarity

When past memories or worries about the future creep into your stream of consciousness, acknowledge them for just a moment. And then, guide yourself back to the present moment. Some people find this coping mechanism easier with the help of a mantra as a cue, such as 'that was all in the past, and now I'm focused on how to improve my present and future.'

It's so common to get stuck in the past simply because of an inbuilt, irrational fear of the unfamiliar. This causes us to turn to ruminate about the past as a subconscious retreat back into the comfort of certainty. This innate human love of certainty is essentially all about survival. We feel the need to feel secure and aware in the attempt to avoid pain and, ideally, find comfort. And what is more certain than that which has already happened? And so, however negative the past may make you feel at times, one thing it doesn't give you is fear or uncertainty. In the same way, moving on from the past, in a sense, means stepping into the unknown future - choosing to leap somewhat blindly the unknown instead of ruminating over the known. It requires the courage to let go of the familiar – which, even when negative can be subliminally comforting to an anxious mind – and allowing yourself to be vulnerable and open to the future.

## The Link Between Memories and Emotion

The other reason it's so difficult to learn how to let go of the past has to do with the way we link emotion to information. They both come from the same part of the brain - the temporal lobe - after all. If you think back to the tragic events of 9/11, you can most likely picture who you were with and what exactly you were doing when you heard about the attack. However, could you recall the 11th June of that same year with the same clarity?

Unless this is also an important day in your personal calendar, then I'm guessing not! Certainly not for every day you have ever lived. This is because our memory is selective when it comes to the details. In order to prioritize meaningful memories from the mundane, our brains don't retain information unless we have feelings attached to it. That's why you may remember fond childhood memories just as clearly as you remember more traumatic past events – but the days where we just did our thing and nothing much happened? Basically – most days we ever live in our lives? They are swiftly forgotten. Maybe even a week after experiencing them!

When information combines with emotion, it creates more of an imprint in your memory. Curiously, some psychologists have also linked this to gender (notice I say gender here – relating to identity and not necessarily to sex chromosomes) as women or anyone with more "feminine" traits have the tendency to attach emotion to more of their memories when compares to their male – or simply more "masculine"-minded – counterparts.

## *Always have a Plan B*

A saying I've gone by since I was young is "failing to prepare is preparing to fail," and harsh as it may sound – it's true! If you feel safe in the knowledge that you have done your research, and always have a plan B in place whenever undertaking a particularly ambitious or risky plan, then a great deal of that anxiety and rumination stemming from the fear of failure will evaporate. Not only that, but focusing your overactive mind on something that is actually constructive to the task at hand, rather than ruminating over what could go wrong, will actually be a great outlet for that nervous mental energy and kill two birds with one stone So I cannot stress this enough – plan, plan and then plan some more!

# Realize you can't predict the future

*Fighting the fear of failure and trusting your instincts over social expectations.*

That being said, you must remember that you cannot - as much as you may believe otherwise - predict the future. Whether it's your career, your relationship, or money worries that are playing on your mind, although you can prepare as best you can to make the best of these things and hope that the future will bring prosperity - we simply cannot know for sure how things will pan out. But don't feel deflated by this - this fact should be liberating! I'm not suggesting you completely throw in the towel and quit caring about the future altogether. However, if you're a chronic overthinker, then you likely worry about things that may not even happen. This is not only a waste of time and mental energy, but it also ruins the present moment! Is it any way to live, constantly looking towards the future with fear and forgetting the blessings you have before you in the present moment?

Just think of all the things you worried about in the past that turned out okay in the long run. Maybe you had similar fears long ago that you can now look back and laugh about. Or alleged failures that you now have the hindsight to realize were necessary to lead you to where you needed to go.

**Fear of Failure**

The fear of failure can be completely debilitating. It can make you question what you're doing and why you're doing it. Fear can cause you to overthink your plans, and hesitate to actually take that first step into action. It can chip away mercilessly at your self-confidence if you let it leave you feeling utterly incapable of taking the action you need in order to accomplish your goals.

That being said, a certain level of fear can also be motivating. As long as you remain focused on what you hope to achieve, and what you need to do in order to get there - compelling yourself to take the leap despite these niggling fearful feelings, then you can use this nervous energy to actually propel yourself forward, towards your goal. And, as already mentioned, when we fail it can actually be a valuable learning experience if we allow it to be. We all must sometimes fail in order to grow as individuals and become better.

## *Take Control over your Thoughts (But Not Too Much!)*

True contentment and freedom require the realization that what goes on inside your head is your own business - no one can affect it unless you let it. This means that you have the final say when it comes to your emotions. Although you can't always predict what will happen outside of yourself, you can take charge of what happens within, and how you react to external stimuli.

I am, of course, not encouraging you to become akin to some sort of unfeeling robot. Bad things happen to the best of us, and we can react however, we see fit - some instances do call for shouting, crying, or taking some time alone and thinking things through. However, we are often self-destructive in our decisions on how to process bad situations. Yes - notice I said "decisions," because although these reactions may seem outside of our control, they really aren't. As I said, the negative reaction in itself may be inevitable, but how you process it is up to you. You have some flexibility to choose in what way you respond to the tragedy. Do you have a tendency to wallow and basque in your grief, isolating yourself from loved ones? Or, do you let rage get the better of you and lash out at others (or towards yourself) due to the sheer frustration of it all?

Regardless of your particular knee-jerk response to a bad mood or day, there is of course, an absolute right or wrong way - just be aware that some coping mechanisms may do more harm than good, only extending the length of time required for you to heal. The important part is that you are aware of the control that you have. With this awareness, whatever challenge arises next, will feel mentally stronger, more grounded to yourself, and less inclined for your overthinking to spiral out of control - opting

instead for more calming and constructive coping mechanisms to your stresses.

That all being said, don't fall into the trap of trying to control your emotions too much. As mentioned, sometimes we all need a good cry or even a good shout - when the occasion calls for it! Pent up emotions or suppressed anger or grief will only linger in your mind until you eventually cannot bottle it up any longer, and it breaks you. Instead, it is better to allow yourself to feel whatever emotions come your way. But make sure you never fully lose touch with your composure or rationality. Express your emotions as a means to communicate or move past them - not simply as a knee-jerk response that will only exacerbate existing worries. Learn to feel your emotions - as you should - but without completely losing your head, so that you can detach yourself from them when the time comes.

## *Treat your Emotions like the Weather*

I like to tell my clients to ride their emotions like the waves that they are - for they will inevitably come and go. The key is to not allow them - whether positive or negative - to completely consume or control you. When I advise controlling your emotions, I don't mean by batting them away and refusing to let them in. Rather, embrace them but then control how you process and move on from them. And remember - just as your negative emotions will come and go, so will your positive ones. Such is the human mind: it never stops! So enjoy your highs, but don't expect them to stay. Be ready for when they are over. But take comfort in the fact that just as your positive emotions are temporary, so are your negative ones - nothing lasts forever - and thank goodness for that! As Ancient Greek Stoic, Seneca wrote:

"They lose the day in expectation of the night, and the night in fear of the dawn."

Indeed, we may not particularly enjoy it when it rains — but we know that this isn't permanent. And so, we may complain - but we put up your umbrella or simply wait indoors for this temporary disturbance to pass. Meanwhile, we are comforted in the knowledge that we will eventually enjoy sunnier days. Our emotions work strangely similar to the weather: both the ups and downs are temporary - to be acknowledged and even responded to with precautionary measures - but always while remembering that no single state will last.

And since the emotions we experience and the ups and downs in our lives aren't permanent in nature, the permanence must come from within. In other words, we must build a reliable level of emotional strength and resilience that will not be weathered by any of life's various storms — even if you do still feel the rain on your skin from time to time!

## Trust Your Instincts

The need for acceptance and thus validation from others is a basic human instinct, stemming from our tribal days where being accepted and liked by the rest of your group could mean the difference between life and death. We all want to fit in, to be liked, respected, and to belong to a community of some sort - whether that's our family, our friendship group, or our workplace. As such, we don't always stay true to who we really are as a sort of self-preservation attempt, causing us to doubt our natural instincts and gut reactions to things. Even if we feel like something was the right choice, we overthink what others may think, what others may have done in our situation - and so it is this failure to trust our instincts and own sense of judgment that often leads us down a path of overthinking.

On top of that, it is quite simply impossible to calculate all possible scenarios in the future for all the challenges you will have to face, so it is important to learn to trust your instincts. This is one of the greatest weapons we have available to us, because we can truly determine what our needs are upfront - without too many deliberations. And, most of the time, it gets us out of trouble without us even realizing it. Sure - we are all fallible and may not always get things right - but if you don't get behind your own ideas and trust in your own abilities, then who else will? Something, a little self-belief, is all we need to dig ourselves out of a rumination pit.

## *You already have everything you need*

Finally, it pays to remember that in this materialistic and appearance-obsessed world, we constantly seek happiness and fulfillment from outside ourselves. This is inherently destructive, as it trains us from a young age to believe that our contentment depends on material possessions or milestones we must all achieve. And of course, a worrying amount of our overthinking stems from these insecurities: around wealth, job prospects, superficial or relationship insecurities. For instance:

"If I earned more money, I'd be happy."

"If I had a different body, I'd be happy."

"If I lived in a bigger house, I'd be happy."

"If I were married, I'd be happy."

Does any of this sound familiar?

I must reiterate: there is no material possession, physical attribute, or social or professional status that will truly change your baseline happiness level - the one that can withstand the rainy days. Sure, they may give you a temporary ego boost making you feel better about yourself for a short period of time, but every single thing that brings superficial joy quickly becomes stale – you soon crave something more.

Think of it this way: remember the last time when you felt completely elated? Maybe just after your first date with someone, when you got your first job, or upon receiving a meaningful compliment from someone you admire. Have you noticed that, despite the warm fuzzy feeling or excitement you may feel from these moments, suddenly, these things aren't enough? We all eventually become blasé about the things that once filled us with joy. However, if you discover how to feel content and at peace with whatever you have right now, in the present moment – even If you acknowledge room for improvement and still retain ample motivation to grow and improve on yourself - you will better establish this baseline of contentment I've been talking about, that isn't so easily shaken by the ups and downs of your life.

On top of this, once you stop punishing yourself for your present circumstances - ruminating over the fact that you should have, or have achieved, X, Y, and Z by now, your desires suddenly seem within reach– as you know you'll be happy regardless, so take the crippling self-inflicted pressure away. Your drive to succeed will now be driven by your self-confidence - and not your self-doubt!

<u>The Bottom Line: Find your Flow and be "in the zone"</u>

Have you ever felt completely consumed by the present moment? Most likely, you are engaged in an activity that you're good at. Something that arouses you jets enough to keep you interested, without typing over into anxious territory. Something that calms you just enough to leave you feeling peaceful, but not so much that it leaves you feeling bored or unstimulated. For some, this could be when painting, drawing, reading, writing, cooking, or running. Whatever it is that gets you into this near-meditative and mind-nourishing state, you will be completely engaged with your present. The back-chatter of your mind begins to melt, and any rogue "what if" thoughts are temporarily silenced, as you enjoy the here and now.

Commonly referred to as being "in the zone," this state of mind is known within psychology as the "flow" state. The term was coined by Hungarian scientist, Mihaly Csikszentmihalyi. He became fascinated with the concept when he studied how artists and musicians become almost entranced by their work. Artists, scientists, and athletes alike all recalled similar experiences when engaged in their activity: a state of both heightened senses and yet seemingly incongruous tranquility.

Indeed, this metaphor of "flow" contributes to the overall imagery of water. Most likely because it is our mental equivalent of floating peacefully down a stream - still moving, but gracefully, at ease, and without your body weighing you down as it would do on land. As put by Bruce Lee:

"You must be shapeless, formless, like water. When you pour water in a cup, it becomes the cup. When you pour water in a bottle, it becomes the bottle. When you pour water in a teapot, it becomes the teapot. Water can drip, and it can crash. Become like water, my friend."

By living in the present, you must assimilate. Become at ease. Although you are alert and often hard at work, you are still relaxed, calm, and ready for wherever the water may take you.

As you strive to let go of your past and quit overthinking your future while you're at it, it helps to also identify something you are aiming for that is greater than yourself. This could be your family, your career development, or even your own mental health or self-discovery journey. Whatever it is, having a motive really does matter. This is what gives us purpose and a reason to continue despite any setbacks or hardships. It reminds us that behind all of the responsibilities, the mistakes, and what-ifs, we are simply flawed, well-intentioned humans trying to get by. No, we can't get it perfect every time. And no - our futures can't be perfect either! But we find the courage and the humility to carry on anyway, trying our best but accepting our mistakes.

And so, we owe it to ourselves to refocus on the present moment. To get out of our heads at least some of the time, and remember to just be - to drink life in as it is currently looking rather than wasting it by mourning what could or should have been.

# Chapter 3

## How to get rid of mental junk

A key part of tackling any overthinking addiction is limiting unnecessary information in the brain and organizing the justified thoughts you are left in a more efficient way. Of course, you must not - and simply cannot - stop thinking altogether. Rather, the secret is to learn how to think with clarity and focus, ditching any mental junk getting in the way of your important thoughts and ideas.

This is where "mental minimalism" comes in. When working on something, it is crucial to liberate the mind from any unnecessary, distracting thoughts. These are the thoughts that can be postponed or set aside for another moment - and so we should jump at that opportunity to clear valuable mental space. We must be more intentional and organized in our thinking, just as we are (or at least, try to!) in other areas of our life - tackling one problem at a time rather than juggling various issues and thus ending up overwhelmed and unable to solve anything whatsoever. Overthinking is also dangerous for our relationships because it implies the inability or refusal to trust other people entirely and to enjoy the moment without unnecessary paranoia. In both cases, excessive thinking and rumination lead to anxiety, frustration, and even invented problems - and so, the focus is lost from the real problems or goals we face.

## Developing a Mental Framework thinking and first principles thinking

One example of "intelligent thinking" in this way is the one explained by Elon Musk about the first principles or about mental framework thinking. So... what on earth is mental framework thinking?

Think of how most companies - not unlike most minds - are largely disorganized and chaotic. Meetings (like your own internal monologues) seem endless and often have no obvious purpose. Initiatives tend to be loosely organized, following protocols and processes (your own habit loops) that follow no real logic. However, "framework thinkers" are able to bring much-needed clarity to their thoughts. Effective frameworks, whether in the workplace or in your own mind, work by drowning out any background noise instead of focusing on the issues and ideas that truly matter. Framework thinkers make more progress and strive for faster and easier solutions. They aren't caught up in the madness.

Here's the thing: there are rarely perfect answers in life, as nothing is black and white; this is why the ability to make faster decisions can often mean the all-important difference between success and failure. As you become someone who establishes frameworks effectively in your own thought processes, you become your own voice of reason in the chaos of your mind.

# Mental Minimalism
*Decluttering your mind.*

So you may have heard of minimalism. This "less is more" movement taking the otherwise materialistic and consumerism world by the storm may not be everyone's cup of tea, but the philosophy behind it certainly lends some food for thought.

Mental minimalism, unlike regular minimalism, has no particular focus on material possessions - rather - it's our mental clutter that needs shedding. The concept asserts that keeping your mind in some sort of order will lead to a more intentional, focused mindset that is both wholesome and gratifying. Mental minimalism is about leaving behind the things that make us stressed and worried - they aren't doing you any favors so let them go. Easier said than done, I know. After giving up on the non-essential or destructive things on your mind, you carve out more time to simply be. To allow yourself to live in the moment. To take in the sensory buffet around you and remember that you are not just these rapid-fire thoughts (more on that later!). Simply put, it is about having less on your mind, but being more.

Downsizing our thoughts right down to the essential means we have to prioritize. This means that boundaries need to be established in order for any of this to work. For instance, if you reply to work emails late at night or at the weekend regularly, your colleagues will expect you to be available at those hours. Or, if you never decline an invitation to go out with friends, even if you're really not up to it and are simply doing it to please them, then they will assume that you always enjoy it, and will always be willing to give them your time and energy. What am I getting at? If we don't set boundaries for ourselves, other people will simply set them for us!

We can't do everything. We can't always say yes, always be there, or always show up. If we want to create time and space for ourselves and free up some precious mental energy, then we have to make room for it. This most likely means saying no sometimes - prioritizing your own mental health or even your own responsibilities over what others want from you. This isn't being selfish - it's being self-compassionate!

# Organizing your mind at work

*Healthy planning and balancing productivity with rest.*

### Quit the multitasking

Here's the thing about focus: despite what many will tell you, you can only focus on one thing at a time. Sure, many will jump between things - focus on one thing for one hour then another thing the next - but to be truly focused, we can only have that one thing on our mind. By incorporating mental minimalism as explained earlier, you are limiting the unnecessary distractions - tossing them out like work-out or unwanted clothes - so that you can see the capsule wardrobe of good quality, desirable pieces that you have left. You may have just three outfits left; you may have fifteen. The important thing is that you have a manageable number for you, enabling you to clearly see what you have to deal with every time you open the closet - then choose one (and only one!) outfit to wear at a time.

## To-do lists are your friend

Your brain, while a biological miracle, still has to work with limited resources. Keeping a concise list of priority tasks each day that need to be accomplished is a great way to be more efficient. If you have a huge pile of tasks before you, it's easy to become overwhelmed, disheartened, or start ruminating about how you'll never get anything done, what will happen then, how terrible everything will be, et cetera… before you realize that if you actually got down to task number one, then in the time you spent overthinking everything, you could have already ticked something off the list!

On top of that, the human brain just loves written lists. They tap into our brain's intrinsic method of organizing itself and processing information. Furthermore, lists are categorical, which coincides with the brain's preference for memorizing things. And if nothing else, seeing the tasks you need to do separated into manageable bitesize chunks is great for your morale, and reminds you that when broken up into steps, you are more than capable of achieving what you need to.

## Learn to disconnect

Modern society is obsessed with technology. After all, it is becoming increasingly harder to live without it - whether it's for pleasure or for work; and whether it's our smartphones or the fact that most jobs now have us chained to our desktops for most of the day. Many mental health experts propose that technology addiction – as in, a chemical and psychological dependence on the stuff – is a reality for millions of people.

This relentless overload of information and screen time is far from healthy, and we all know it but often choose to ignore it. The brain must have the chance to reflect, refresh and re-energize. A constant stream of incoming data is harmful - perhaps even more than we already realize - as it goes against the natural makeup and functioning of the human brain. This is especially apparent in the evening, as many of us have replaced our healthy bedtime reading rituals for endless scrolling of our social media news feeds until the early hours - not only overstimulating the brain making it even harder to shut down for sleep, but the blue light behind the screen actually inhibits the production of the sleep hormone, melatonin, as our primitive brains read this as sunlight - meaning we are not only frying our brains but not even allowing them the medicine of good quality sleep.

Do you know how your smartphone or computer overheats and crashes from time-to-time when it's been running for too long? The same concept applies to our brains. Sometimes they just need to be turned off for a little while before we restart them.

## Take enough breaks

So we've established like any other advanced machine, your brain still has limited energy supplies at any one time. As such, we can't expect it always to work at full capacity. We wouldn't expect this of any computer - and yet we inflict this expectation on ourselves - when not only do we have the same limited energy issue, but also other complications like emotions and willpower thrown into the mix! The brain is similar to a machine in this sense: the more information that is processed, the more energy is consumed. And so, by constantly processing information - which could be studying for an exam, but it could also be simply talking to someone, or yes - overthinking while all by yourself.

These may not seem like particularly tiring tasks, but your brain begs to differ. You know that sound your computer makes (at least, if it is as old as mine is) and it makes that whirring sound? You can almost feel its discomfort. This is when you get that slightly guilty feeling - maybe you downloaded too many things or clicked a few too many times, and it got overloaded. Well, maybe extend this concern for the most valuable computer you'll ever own - the one between your ears!

Simply put, you can't expect to fire off thoughts for hours and maintain the same efficiency level. And so, breaks are absolutely fundamental for your brain.

## Use a calendar

According to neuroscientists, keeping a calendar or schedule is an unbeatable method for externalizing your memories, thus allowing you to free up space in your brain. If you can make a quick note of where you need to be and when, then why use up precious brain space to hold onto this piece of information, cluttering other items that are perhaps more necessary to be uploaded onto your mental harddrive?.

Whether you prefer to download an app, use Outlook, or just get a good old-fashioned "flip" calendar like the one your mother probably adorns on her fridge (hey, she knows what she's doing) - habitually using and referring a calendar is a hugely underrated way to make your life become much easier and less stressful.

Get enough good-quality sleep

It's strange to think that until the 1950s, sleep was a largely misunderstood phenomenon. We just knew that at night, we eventually get tired and fall asleep until the morning. Today, however, scientists know that sleep is a crucial part of maintaining healthy brain function. When we don't get enough sleep, numerous problems arise: from concentration to hand-eye coordination, to memory loss and mood instability. I'm sure we've all been there at some point and can vouch for these claims personally...

Scientists generally agree that a minimum of seven hours of sleep is necessary for adults. But it's not only the quantity but also the quality that you need to be aware of. For many of us, we can just tell from waking up whether we had what we call "a good night's sleep" or not... Sleep gives a chance for your brain to reorder itself. Temporarily free from the burden of your constant daytime demands and thought processes - it begins the night shift. Essentially, it sifts through the thoughts you had that day - the jury is still out when it comes to the precise workings of the mind during slumber - it's mysterious in that way - but what we do know is that it doesn't stop. Far from it - MRI scans have proven that the brain is hard at work even when your consciousness switches off. And science also tells us that our brain function deteriorates dramatically the longer we go sleep-deprived - so let's do it a favor and just let it do its thing, okay?

## Never Stop Learning

Here's another thing that neuroscience has discovered about our brains: it continues to reshape itself throughout life - even throughout adulthood. It was once believed that the brain stopped developing after adolescence or young adulthood. However, we now know that our brains actually continue to change over the course of your entire lifetime - depending, of course, on how we nourish it.

When you learn something new - whatever it is - your brain creates new connections. It could be how to speak a new language, or simply a new recipe. But over time of practicing this new skill, reinforcing the new connections we built, these new connections gradually work to change the overall structure of this particular part of your brain. Scientists call this phenomenon "neuroplasticity". The significance of its discovery tells us more about our capacity for learning and how to heal traumatic injuries and neurological diseases.

We really underestimated our brains for some time, but if we feed them well (with sleep, rest, and learning), then they truly blossom.

# How overthinking ruins relationships
*Avoid thinking your problems into existence*

Overthinking and the mental junk accumulated, as a result, can damage your relationship more than you can probably even imagine. Relationships of any kind are complicated enough as they are. After all, humans are complicated - and for two to get along without too much fuss and while establishing boundaries, trust, and maybe, even love and mutual understanding - can be a complete minefield especially, if at least one party is an overthinker, with limited mental clarity thanks to their piles of mental junk not letting them see straight. Of course, I am not encouraging you to simply wash your hands of all of life's causes for concern or preoccupation; To deny any real issues your relationship may have, for example. However, incessant worrying will only do more harm than good - not actually solving your problems while giving you even more to worry about as your overworked brain causes additional trouble!

In one study, 40 different couples completed questionnaires to determine their overall relationship satisfaction. The catch? Half of the couples were asked to analyze the relationship before completing the questionnaire. They had to 'list all the reasons why your relationship with your dating partner is going the way it is, and to take time to analyze why it is good or bad.' Then, immediately after analyzing their relationships in this straight-to-the-point fashion, they completed the questionnaire. Meanwhile, the control group simply answered the satisfaction questionnaire without this step of first analyzing their relationship.

All couples in both groups were then contacted between four and eight months later to determine whether they were still together. And do you know what happened? The couples in the control group (who skipped the analysis part) demonstrated a strong correlation between how satisfied they claimed to be in the questionnaire, and whether or not they separated when contacted several months later. In other words, self-reported happier couples were more likely to have stayed together. Predictable so far.

However, for the couples who were asked to analyze their relationships in detail before answering the questionnaire about relationship satisfaction, there was almost no correlation between how happy they reported being, and whether or not they went their separate ways. Essentially, the way they felt about their relationships after this rigorous analysis was completely unrelated to whether or not they ended up staying together. This is because analyzing their relationship beforehand had actually created confusion just in time for the questionnaire that followed - they may have overthought their relationship to the point that they had fabricated problems that then seeped into their questionnaire answers. Essentially, the pre-analysis had left participants scrambled and led to the questionnaire being a much less accurate measurement for compatibility.

What can we determine from this? Quite simply, overthinking - though you may think since it suggests thinking a lot, it may pay off in some way - actually reduces mental clarity.

So why does over-analysis often only lead to more confusion in this way? One possible reason is that it causes us to believe that we have a deeper insight than we actually do - and that we must pay more attention to these alleged insights rather than our actual behavior. Therefore, rather than only taking how you and your partner interact with each other as an indicator of whether or not your relationship will last, you unwittingly fabricate thoughts and theories that actually distance you away from the facts.

On top of that, many of our behaviors and preferences are actually unconscious. As a result, we don't even know the true sources of our feelings. All we know is that we feel them and then come up with reasoning - yet the problem is it is often difficult to assess the validity of our own emotions... And so, we try to make sense of it all by making up rational explanations concerning the other person involved. They must be wrong, or irrational, not me—but these explanations are not accurate. Our emotions are especially complex and often irrational. Consequently, attempting to apply rational tactics to determine why we feel a certain way can create even more confusion about our emotional state.

Additionally, we are also pretty bad when it comes to predicting our emotional reactions to future events. We typically overestimate the strength and duration of future emotional responses, whether positive and negative. We overthink how things will feel, exaggerating them in the process. You will most likely have noticed it - when the anticipation of something turns out to be more intense than the emotions you feel when the moment you've been waiting for actually comes. This also applies to our relationships, as we tend to overestimate how happy we will be to enter into a relationship with someone, or even how unhappy we will be following a breakup. This effect seems to be particularly driven by our tendency to imagine the extremes in our overthinking. We blow things way out of proportion in our minds. This habitual overestimation of our future emotional responses occurs because when we think towards a potential future event, we forget that it wouldn't exist in isolation. In other words, your relationship may end, but you'll still have your job, routine, friends, and other things that bring joy, purpose, or satisfaction to your life. Furthermore, we tend to underestimate our future selves' emotional resilience: we can actually deal with a lot more than we tend to give ourselves credit for.

So, how can you give a relationship the best possible chance at success? Firstly, don't overthink or over-analyze it: nothing is perfect, and if you magnify every minute doubt or perceived flaw, you will never find happiness. Secondly, when assessing the potential impact of the break-up, think more broadly about how your future would look - with all the rest of your current life intact. You may still feel grief and a degree of sadness, of course. But your life is more than your relationship, and your resilience is a lot stronger than you think it is.

## The Bottom Line: Time For a Mental Clear-Out!

Before the age of 50, Elon Musk has now innovated and built three ground-breaking multi-billion-dollar companies in completely different fields. At first glance, you would be forgiven for linking his rapid success, his proven ability to solve seemingly unsolvable problems, and his creativity to his unbreakable work ethic. No doubt, work ethic plays an important role in succeeding and reaching the heights of your potential — but there's more to it than that. Look around - or maybe in the mirror: there are unfailingly dedicated and hardworking people who can currently not even dream of such achievement. And for most of us, we never will. What then, you may ask, is the missing jigsaw piece for the vast majority of us?

Some of the most world-changing and incredible minds of all time to date — from Aristotle, to Marie Curie, to Thomas Edison— you could say, incorporate a missing link to marry together their curiosity and enthusiasm for learning, complex problem-solving and creativity. This missing link actually has relatively little to do with how hard they work; rather, it's about how they think. The most successful people - however diverse - tend to have one major thing in common: the practice of actively questioning every assumption they possess - and not taking anything a given. You may think you 'know' about a given problem or scenario — just as people throughout history thought they "knew" that the world was flat or that children cannot feel pain... Quitting overthinking doesn't mean quitting curiosity, questioning or reason. Usually, when we're faced with complex problems, we aim to tackle it like we imagine as everybody else would, or how we deem is the normal response. "First-principles thinking" is a powerful way to help you

break free from this limiting herd mentality; think outside the box and innovate new solutions to familiar problems. But of course, to hope for such clarity and creativity - we must throw out all the mental junk first!

# Chapter 4

>>>———————————<<<

## I'm not my thoughts, I'm what I do

For many of my overthinking clients, it's hard to separate this habit from their personality. This means that you actually cease to see overthinking as a habit that can be stopped, but you actually view it as an integral part of your personality. You perhaps cannot imagine a version of yourself that doesn't excessively ruminate over things in this way. Once this mindset is in place, the overthinking habit becomes worryingly fixes it in place. But not because the client is correct in thinking in this way! Rather, as soon as we see something as "just how it is" or "simply the way I am," it becomes a sort of self-fulfilling prophecy where the individual overthinks about how they overthink, and so, the cycle continues. If you don't believe you can be helped, then not much can be done.

However, once you see overthinking and rumination as the bad habit that it is, to which anyone is susceptible, then you realise that you can overcome it and still be you - just a mentally healthier and less anxious version.

Now for some advice on the correct habits to have if you want to try to think less, worry less, and be more productive in life. I want to talk about the importance of a pre-established routine so that we don't have to waste time and go crazy thinking about what to do every day because everything will already be decided at the beginning.

# Changing your habits
*The importance of daily routine and physical health.*

## Your Overthinking Isn't Who You Are

The trouble is, rumination gives you a warped, pessimistic perspective on yourself and the way your life is panning out. Overthinking also drains your mental resources, which can interfere with your judgment and ability to problem-solve. As a result, you end up caught in a tangle of self-destructive or self-flagellating thoughts, and yet no insight or clarity is gained. Instead, rumination only makes you feel worse about whatever is on your mind.

Introverts, especially, need quiet time for self-reflection and introspection, because they are often more sensitive to everything around them, they crave downtime, without distraction or interruption from the outside world, to process the stuff of the day—the interactions, their reactions to them, and simply to think their thoughts. Introspection is about self-growth, looking inward in order to learn from the challenges we're facing.

It is essential to be in tune with your own physical and mental state in order to understand why you are overthinking and how you can stop it. Here are some concrete tips on how to get there:

**The Importance of Sleep**

Overthinking at night is largely down to the brain processing what has happened to us during the day. Since our days now present us with such a lot of stimuli - we're communicating more and taking in and processing more information - we don't allow for gaps in order to process our thoughts during the daytime.

We don't have the time and space during the day to process what's happened and to evaluate and make sense of it. Sometimes the only opportunity we get to do this is when we're in bed, trying to get some precious sleep. A lot of clients tell me that as soon as their head hits the pillow and they close their eyes, all their niggling thoughts start coming out of the shadows – suddenly remembering all the things that may have been lying dormant in the back of their mind throughout the day.

On top of that, this is a vicious cycle of rumination and insomnia, as night-time rumination hinders sleep while lack of sleep actually increases stress levels, and thus your tendency to be anxious and overthink things throughout your day. So overall, we should all be prioritizing sleep. Adults should be getting at least seven or eight hours a night. The importance of our sleeping habits regarding our mental clarity and overall well-being cannot be underestimated. After all, we spend around a third of our lives sleeping, which should be seen as the catalyst for making the other two thirds successful, rewarding and energized. We cannot hope to perform our best or even think with clarity when our perception is clouded by the physical and mental exhaustion inflicted by sleep deprivation.

## "Eat the frog first"

Here's a great habit that can change your life for the better: strive always to do your worst task first thing in the morning. Every single day, you've got one major to-do that you know should be your top priority - but despite this, it can often be the most difficult one to start. On top of that, when you've got the whole day ahead of you, it's easy to just put things off "until later" - after that meeting, or after running that errand. You may think since you are not a "morning person", or you feel so tired and unmotivated first thing in the morning, you feel the need to ease yourself in by starting with easier tasks, and putting off whatever you may be dreading to the afternoon.

However, this only gives you the opportunity to ruminate over this less appealing item on your to-do list for the whole day. And worse still - if you keep telling yourself "not yet" or "I'll come back to it later," - the chances are, you will end up eventually telling yourself "not today" and "I'll deal with this tomorrow." So that's a whole day wasted while you put off this task, only to then repeat this same twisted routine the very next day. We all know this isn't logical, and yet we kid ourselves into thinking we are being kind to ourselves by putting ourselves through this mental torture and willpower gymnastics. It would have been a lot kinder to rip off the bandaid or swallow the pill as soon as we could - to save ourselves the burden!

By "worst" task, this could either be the hardest, or it could even be the most important thing on your agenda, which is making you feel uneasy for whatever reason. Whatever it is that you are procrastinating, as touched upon earlier, our anticipation of negative feelings is often completely exaggerated. In other words, most often, whatever we are dreading most likely isn't so bad once we bite the bullet. So at the risk of parroting a well-known sportswear brand, just do it; before you can do anything else to distract yourself, before you have time to think about it too much.

Mark Twain notoriously called this strategy "eating your frog." He declared that if the first thing you do each morning is "eat a live frog," then you can go through the rest of the day comforted in the knowledge that the worst is already behind you. Your own "frog" is the task you are most dreading. By jumping in and crossing this off straight away, the rest of your day will seem easier and more manageable.

First thing in the morning your mind is clear, the world is only just waking up, and so your attention likely hasn't yet been pulled into six different directions. This is your one opportunity to prioritize the thing that matters to you most before other responsibilities and distractions start to pile up. And, by ticking off something important on your to-do list before anything else, you get both the required momentum and a sense of achievement - all before 10 am!

And so, set yourself up to eat your frog tomorrow morning last thing before you call it a day tonight. Identify tomorrow's frog - and write it down on a post-it or notepad that you'll see when you return to your desk in the morning. If you can, gather together whatever materials you'll need to get it done and have that out, too, so that all you'll have to do tomorrow is get your nose stuck in it. Getting things done efficiently and without unnecessary fuss and overthinking is a great habit to instill, and if you start each day by accomplishing something important, you'll feel like a small weight has lifted before you're even in the thick of your day. This little boost you will get will only spur you on to achieve more and more, causing your productivity to snowball. **Leverage Your Unique Energy Levels**

The key to stepping out of this overthinking mode is focusing on increasing your productivity. Keeping your mind busy with more tangible tasks is a surefire way to keep any niggling doubts and insecurities threatening your inner peace at bay. And this kind of sustainable productivity, unshaken by the storms brewing in your head, can be achieved by leveraging your own natural energy levels. This may sound pretty abstract, but seizing the ebbs and flows of your natural energy levels is about understanding yourself; observing and acknowledging the natural patterns and rhythm of your body's energy flow - both the surges and the dips - and thus harnessing your energy peaks when they occur.

Your ultradian rhythms are your body's natural cycles of energy and are key to maintaining motivation and stamina. Just like the tides, sometimes your energy levels are more powerful and gushing, and sometimes they temporarily recede. It's all-natural and nothing to try to fix or correct, but to embrace.

Many people senselessly try to push through a task, whipping their body and mind into submission, even when they are mentally exhausted and haven't got any more creative input to offer. This is a highly damaging and counterproductive - you can't pour from an empty cup, after all. Or pour from an empty cup. We can only be productive when our reserves are replenished - that means getting enough sleep, food, and water - but it also means having sufficient mental and emotional breaks too. Or choosing to rest or carry out a more basic task when you naturally have lower energy levels, leaving your most challenging tasks to when you feel mentally capable. Understanding your own energy cycles and taking advantage of your energy bursts while acknowledging when your energy is at a natural low. Thus, incorporating some deliberate rest will ultimately make you more productive - and of course, less stressed.

Getting through an entire workday while maximizing your productivity requires breaks throughout the day to account for these ebbs and flows. If you refuse to take adequate breaks, then you will only make more errors, experience more stress and fatigue, and mess up your immune, nervous, and endocrine (hormone) systems. So this is serious stuff!

These frequent breaks don't have to be long or elaborate. Something as quick and simple as taking a quick stroll in a nearby park, or taking a few minutes to stretch or meditate could be just the step back you need to then return to your task feeling brimming with motivation and ideas again. Whatever type of break you choose, be disciplined about it. During this period of mental rest, try not to let thoughts about your tasks creep into your consciousness - you'll have plenty of time for that later! But you will only reap the benefits of your break if you allow yourself to truly disconnect from your worries and responsibilities. There's no skipping this important step if you want to get some quality work done at all today. It's like refueling your creativity - don't expect to just have fresh ideas on tap at all hours if you don't even stop to recharge!

# Changing your environment
*Giving your mind a break! It will thank you.*

It is said while Albert Einstein was in the process of formulating his groundbreaking theory of relativity, he achieved his greatest lightbulb-moment breakthrough while taking a short break from working to relax by a fire and let his mind rest.

Not only does this support the argument that breaks are a help and not a hindrance to productivity, but also that changes in environment can be just what you need to encourage new ways of thinking. Sometimes, we remain at our desks and push ourselves until we can't give anymore – but it's not until we finally give in and take a walk, or even just go for a bathroom break or get up to open a window, that the answer we've been racking our brain for comes to us. Why does this happen? Because our brains get quickly bored. When we focus on one thing for too long, it becomes less and less clear. Eventually, we lose focus of the task – but this only tends to make us even more frustrated with ourselves – and so we overthink, we push too hard, and thus, the vicious cycle continues...

If you find yourself overthinking, or struggling to think straight and achieve focus, simply change your environment. Go to a coffee shop, take a quick walk in a park or, simply shift your attention on another task for a while. You could give the computer a rest and switch to pencil and paper. Or simply stop thinking about the problem for a moment, and just allow yourself to daydream. They say that many of our most creative thoughts come to us while in the shower. Well, this is why. Allowing ourselves to temporarily move away from our daily responsibilities and letting our minds wander is often when we inadvertently stumble upon the jackpot. A kettle watched never boils!

## Focus on one single task

As mentioned in the last chapter, multitasking is a lie. We may be able to go back and forth between tasks, but this is usually no help, and only further scrambles our thoughts and stresses us out even more.

Richoteting between different tasks or projects may seem to keep things exciting, or even make you believe you are being more productive and efficient by tackling more than one thing at once. However, in truth, this habit doesn't do you or your productivity any favors. Instead, although focusing on just one task for a long period of time may be difficult – especially with smartphones by our sides most of the time – practicing "single-tasking," as in, taking your tasks one at a time and devoting your attention fully to each one until it is complete, can help to rebuild your focus and attention span and keep any overthinking and procrastination at bay.

According to a Harvard study carried out in 2010, we spend 46.9% of our time thinking about something other than what we're actually doing in that given moment. And this habitual mental time-travel prevents us from enjoying the present, having a great impact on both our ability to relax, and to feel contented.

Concentrating solely on just one task for a long duration of time can be testing, especially with smartphones in our hand and our eyes fixated on a screen of some sort for most of our waking hours. However, practicing "single-tasking" can help to rebuild both your capacity to your focus, and attention span overall. It's less mentally overwhelming and more natural for your mind to focus on one thing at a time, and you're more likely to tap into your flow state, which Mihaly Csikszentmihalyi describes as the 'secret to happiness.'

Therefore, you can also use this as a mind trick to avoid incessant rumination. Next time you are struggling with anxious, racing thoughts, try singling out one particular task - no matter how seemingly trivial in the scheme of things - such as tidying your workspace or doing your laundry. This can not only serve as a great distraction from your racing mind, as it forces you to fill your consciousness with the straightforward task at hand, but it also chips away at the pile of things at the back of your mind you feel you need to do. Once the simple stuff is out of the way, it is as though you clear mental space to tackle the bigger things on your mind.

## The Importance of Action (Step by Step)

Often, when we discuss goals - whether it's to make more money, to lose weight, or to build a business - we talk about the bigger

actions. I often sing the praises of taking concrete action to see results myself.

However, although this leap into action is the crux of short-term achievements, it is consistency that will set you up for long-term success. Here is the problem: Every action cis presented with resistance. We may want to start that business but we may have to give up the security of our job. We may want to live a healthier life, but our temptations present a real psychological resistance. We may want to improve our mental health and well-being, and yet our stubborn thoughts continue to race around our minds, threatening to sabotage any such goals...

Even by just taking that first small step action, we need to break through the resistance of our procrastination, our lack of self-confidence or self-efficacy, or the resistance of that critical voice in the back of our minds telling us our goals are ridiculous. To overcome our personal resistances, we need copious amounts of mental energy. And as already discussed, our level of mental energy is not constant - we have peaks and troughs even throughout a single day. Sometimes we feel like the world is our oyster, and other times we feel completely defeated.

## *Set your own standards; Be your own motivator*

This is a key reason why people depend heavily on external motivation. That is: allowing the promise of others' praise, or the fear of their disapproval spur you forward, rather than allowing your own inner voice to keep you moving. We all know that it's best to be our own motivators - but sometimes we don't feel like this is enough - even though this is the only sustainable option. External motivators can be fickle - people's reactions can be unpredictable, and you may become enslaved by the worry of what others think about you - whether it's your boss, your partner, or your mother! We all are striving to please someone else through our actions - but really, we should be striving to please ourselves above all else. This way, we can know for sure if

we made ourselves proud. We aren't always waiting to see what someone else thinks.

This external dependence is why people often start with something big and always slip off after sometimes—for instance, going from never working out to starting to do so for 3 hours a day. Or forcing yourself to write 10,000 on your first day trying to write the novel you've always dreamed of writing. We pick these goals out of thin air - maybe because that's what your friend or your colleague, or someone you saw on Instagram is doing… But our goals need to be tailored to our own abilities, needs, and aspirations!

And what tends to happen in these kinds of copy-cat scenarios? The first day or two is such a stretch, and so unnatural for our usual routine, that we fail to produce enough mental energy to resist the temptation to give up altogether. We could have tried just a 3 hours working out spread over a week, to begin with, or only writing the first 1000 words in your first day of writing - this would have been more sustainable, would have given you the little high needed to maintain your motivation levels, and would have been the first small steps into a huge achievement. It seems like a no-brainer, and yet many of us feel so motivated at the beginning that we break off more than we can chew, and then end up packing it in altogether.

### The Bottom Line: You're not your thoughts, you're what you do

The more we think about thoughts, the more we think about how bizarre it is to think. To overthink. To think about how you wished you didn't overthink. And to then realize you're overthinking it.

The thing about thoughts is that they emerge from your consciousness inadvertently, to then slip away as easily as they appear to make room for the next one. This is how our brain has functioned from as long as we have been able to think. We can't imagine not thinking because even that requires thinking. And so, this is so natural to us, we don't even… think about it.

To pin your identity to your thoughts is misleading since they come about in an uncontrollable way. This is why so many struggle with intrusive thoughts - when unwanted thoughts or compulsions repeatedly pop up in one's mind, and they feel completely unable to overcome them or stop them from entering their consciousness. Many believe that these bad thoughts make them a bad person, or that thinking certain things makes them crazy. But we cannot control what pops into our mind! In fact, the more we worry about something popping into our mind, the more it pops up.

I guess what I'm getting at is that the more we think about something, the longer it lingers in your mind. So if we are thinking about unpleasant things, or things we wished we didn't think about so much, then they will inevitably only outstay their welcome even longer. It's easier said than done to simply stop thinking about something. The more we try, the more impossible it becomes. But by using techniques to break out of this overthinking cycle altogether, we can not only free ourselves from this prison of rumination, freeing up mental space and energy for more worthwhile, pleasant and productive matters, but we also learn that we are not our thoughts, but rather our actions.

As author Eckhart Tolle states:

"Be present as the watcher of your mind — of your thoughts and emotions as well as your reactions in various situations. Be at least as interested in your reactions as in the situation or person that causes you to react."

To overthink and ruminate about disempowering thoughts only reinforces them in your mind. And so, to overcome the burden of overthinking, pay attention to your thoughts by being mindful of your mental landscape - what could be triggering it in your environment or your emotional state - and intercept them before they get the chance to wreak havoc. You may not be able to control your thoughts - but you can control how you react to them!

# Chapter 5

## Perfectionism vs excellence

We are often taught that if we want to get results, we have to strive for perfection: perfect skills, perfect self-discipline, and perfect actions. But this is unrealistic and a harmful expectation to impose on ourselves. Whether you are a perfectionist with your work, your health and fitness level, your relationship, your looks, or any other way that you rank your success in your life - it only sets us up for a life of sweating the small stuff, overthinking ourselves into oblivion, and sabotaging our own satisfaction and even - ironically - our success.

And yet, despite the growing body of research revealing that perfectionism puts you at a greater risk of anxiety, depression, and even heart problems, many of us still believe perfectionism is a positive attribute. Sometimes, we get trapped in a vicious cycle of toxic perfectionism, where we set ourselves a target so challenging to reach that it is unrealistic, and yet the perfectionist within pushes you to the absolute mental, physical, and emotional limit in order to give all you have in the name of this ill-founded goal. The result? We wind up working ourselves to the bone, and yet still believing ourselves to have "underachieved."

We must learn that sometimes imperfection is often natural, expected, and nothing to be afraid of. For instance, you may have gotten one question in an exam wrong, but still excelled overall. Is this reason to berate yourself? Of course not! Be glad that you excelled, and learn from that one mistake you made. This is why we must aim for excellence rather than perfection. To strive for overall success and happiness - and not a life or career absolutely free from mistakes or obstacles.

Perfectionism is ultimately a self-defeating way to live your life. It is built on the painful irony: that making mistakes - as well as admitting them and allowing yourself to move past them - is a necessary part of growing up and being a human being in this world. With every mistake, you learn something about how to do better next time - whether it regards your career, your relationships, or your life overall. By avoiding mistakes at all costs, you are essentially wrapping yourself up in cotton wool to avoid all potential risk - and this is actually hindering your personal growth and self-development by not allowing yourself to aim high, regardless of the obstacles you will inevitably face along the way.

Perfectionism has also been linked to a whole host of health issues, such as depression, anxiety, self-harm, eating disorders, obsessive-compulsive disorder (OCD), insomnia, heart problems, chronic headaches, and - most tragically of all, early mortality and suicide. And so I must reiterate, no one should ever try or even want to be perfect. Life is so much more than that!

## *Where does perfectionism come from?*

Perfectionism is a result of social conditioning, established in mind from childhood. Parents, teachers, and other adults in your early life can easily, and perhaps unwittingly, imprint this attitude that anything less than perfection is failure. Just think back to how you were likely graded at school. Or how you may have tried to impress your teachers or parents by getting everything right. Of course, some children succumb to this more than others, but for many - perfectionist or not - we grow up believing that there's a right way and a wrong way, and that every failure tarnishes our self-worth somehow. Exactly what perfection entails is often nebulous and ends up being what the adult says it is.

Of course, it wasn't your parents' or your teacher's fault - this is simply how society currently functions - and how they will have been conditioned too. We all go through life believing success to be this rigid binary that we either master or miss altogether.

This perhaps explains why the crux of perfectionism is "external locus of control," which simply means that someone seeks validation - which in this case is the confirmation of perfection - from outside of oneself. Even if someone holds their own standard of perfection, this standard stems from the adults around them while growing up. It is not usually a standard that was consciously, intelligently, and maturely chosen after some level of deliberate thought.

Perfectionism, by definition, suggests a standard both unrealistic and also based on an external measure. Therefore, the first step to overcome perfectionism is the recognition that these standards are external; They aren't based on your own values and ideals but on someone else's that have somehow been instilled in you. Think about it: a lot of what we do - consciously or not - is to impress others. If you focus on what you really want and expect instead, you can save yourself a lot of unnecessary pressure, and have more clarity about what success looks like to you.

For instance, was it your parents who instilled the idea in you that owning a detached property and being married with two kids before 35 is what success looks like? Was it your social circle that made you believe that success means working in a high-rise office building in the inner-city sending emails all day? Or, maybe it's the online content you consume that makes you see success as having a toned physique, or traveling the whole world before you "settle down"?

Whatever you may have been led to believe success must look like for you, it's best to be your own author - to come up with your own ideals and dreams, rather than basing them on other's standards. This alignment between your true ambitions and your actions is the closest anyone can get to perfection! And since this looks so different to every individual, the whole concept of perfection becomes obsolete anyway...

Of course, even your own internal standards can be highly unrealistic, likely still influenced at least somewhat by your past and who you spend your time with. Just remember that constantly striving to be "the best" causes increased stress and anxiety - only reducing your chances of performing well. By adopting a more casual approach, you inflict less tension and pressure on yourself, and your performance will likely improve.

## *Why we are so Obsessed with Perfection*

And so, culturally, we still often regard perfectionism as a positive. Even saying you have perfectionistic tendencies is regarded as a coy form of self-promotion or "humble brag." So much so that it's practically become the stock answer to the fateful "What's your greatest weakness?" job interview question.

And admittedly, some researchers propose that there is an adaptive - or 'healthy' - form of perfectionism, characterized by setting high standards for yourself, self-motivation and self-discipline. However, there is also a maladaptive, 'unhealthy' version - when your best just never seems to be good enough, and not meeting goals frustrates you to the point that you berate yourself or even end up loathing or harming yourself. And while research shows that these more maladaptive and self-destructive perfectionist attributes may make you more susceptible to chronic anxiety and depression, other studies show that 'adaptive' perfectionist traits like striving for achievement and pushing yourself to accomplish your goals have no effect at all, or may even protect you from such mental problems by giving you a sense of purpose and direction.

# Doing the right thing vs. doing the things right

*Strive for Excellence, Not Perfection*

So how can you switch from a perfectionist mindset to an excellent one?

Pursuers of excellence value themselves by who they are, and strive for the best - but when they fail, they pick themselves up, see the positives of the experience, and learn from their mistakes. Perfectionists, on the other hand, when they run into difficulty, become easily overwhelmed and often give up once a perfect outcome no-longer seems likely. Pursuers of excellence experience setbacks and temporary disappointment, of course, but they keep going anyway - viewing themselves as more than simply their past achievements. They focus on the present - what they can do now to make tomorrow better. Perfectionists obsess over past mistakes and ruminate over worries for tomorrow, so tend to overlook what they can do to be productive in the here and now.

Perfectionists feel they must always come out on top and be the best. Anything less, and they feel disappointed. However, pursuers of excellence don't compare their achievements to those of others in this way, recognizing that we each are on our own journey, and must only compare ourselves today with who we were yesterday. This goes to show why perfectionists hate criticism, and often cannot cope unless they receive nothing but praise, treating any commentary less than complete awe as evidence that they have failed. However, pursuers of excellence see criticism as a way to learn and are more open in general to others' opinions and ideas - as they are more adaptive and less blinkered to their own specific perspective and expectations.

Overall, perfectionists have to win or get things 100% right to maintain high self-esteem. Pursuers of excellence, however, can still feel good within themselves; however, a particular challenge or task turned out. They will always keep striving to do better next time - but remain content with where they're at right now.

And so, as you will now understand, there is a clear difference between being a perfectionist and excellent. Having said that, what would you prefer to be? Later in the chapter, I will give you useful tips to put into practice to harness your unique kind of excellence.

## *Tactical Thinking versus Strategic Thinking*

This "perfection" versus "excellence" paradigm is comparable to the concept of tactical versus strategic thinking. Tactical thinkers are those who tend to focus on "doing things right," whereas strategic thinkers are more concerned with "doing the right things" the way they perceive it. As you can imagine - like the perfectionist, the tactical thinker sees tasks as a list of rules to be followed. There's no room for flexibility, adaption, or human error is you're a perfectionist tactical-thinking person! It might sound like these are the people who have it together - but life cannot be lived in this way! And even the most high-level work cannot be carried out in this way. It's narrow-minded, unsustainable, and glosses over the fact that we are human - and both adaptation and some mistakes here and there are part and parcel of how we do things.

Doing the right things by the book involves doing things obediently and efficiently. However, this may not be enough; the most successful people aren't those who spend their lives following rules and living their every decision by some pre-decided guidelines set out by someone else. No, a leader is someone who uses their own intellect and capacities to decide to do the most appropriate according to the specific situation. This is called being strategic. If you want to be innovative and do something that others have not yet done, then being a perfectionist, or merely a tactical thinker, will not be enough.

# The Link Between Anxiety and Perfectionism

*Lower your standards; increase your quality of life.*

As discussed earlier, our anxiety - that heart-racing, nausea-inducing panic or dread we feel - sometimes just by thinking alone - is a result of our age-old fight-or flight stress response. This neurophysiological reaction is what jerks us into gear and prepares us for what our bodies believe is a life-or-death situation - an attack, or a fight. As also discussed, this biological hype-up we may feel every time we think of all the work we have to get done tomorrow, or about giving that presentation next week serves us no purpose today other than to make sure we get no sleep, lose our appetite, and have basically every bodily function - from our circulation right down to our reproductive system - suffer tremendously as a result.

It perhaps comes as no shock, then, that perfectionism alone can fuel this fire of anxiety. This obsession with getting things a certain way, never being happy with what you have and always striving for bigger, better, more - will only harm you both mentally and physically in the long run. Yes - this is a perfectionist's nightmare - as the more you strive for perfection, the more imperfectly your body and mind can function...

So, as you can perhaps now imagine, your perfectionism may well be fanning the flames of your anxiety and overthinking. However, through some careful practice and work on your self-awareness, you may be able to "loosen up" a little to get a better handle on your perfectionism - as well as the anxious and overthinking tendencies that often come with it! Here are some pointers on where to begin:

**Overcome your negative thoughts:** Perfectionism is often fueled by habitual negative thoughts. You can get past this way of thinking through techniques such as writing exercises and positive affirmations. Quieting your negative thoughts about perfectionism can also help you to remain realistic and self-forgiving about what you set out to accomplish.

**Build your self-esteem:** Perfectionism often has a harmful impact on your self-esteem. This is because if you tend to evaluate your own sense of self-worth according to the flawlessness of your performance, then your self-esteem is doomed to plummet as soon as these lofty expectations are not met. Combine this with the fact that a perfectionist's goals are often unrealistic in the first place, and you set yourself up for avoidable disappointment. Rather being so self-critical, channel this energy into elevating your self-esteem, however that may look for you. For example, allowing yourself to rest and recharge (including your mind!), focusing on your strengths and abilities rather than any weaknesses or perceived limitations, practicing self-care, and finding ways to support others who could use your help.

**Limit stress:** Perfectionist tendencies can be a fundamental contributor to your daily stress levels. Persistent stress can drain energy, increase your overthinking, and fuel any anxiety and depression you may be dealing with. So make every effort to release yourself from the stress over your irrational obsession with perfectionism by constantly reminding yourself that perfect isn't real, and things don't have to be 100% as you planned them in order for them to be excellent. Of course, some stress will often still remain. But you can better manage these other challenges in your life if things not being perfect isn't a cause!

# How to be a perfect imperfectionist
*How to be productive but stop chasing "perfect."*

And so, those who strive for perfection may think they are simply being ambitious or determined, but they often only unwittingly deprive themselves of contentment and life satisfaction, no matter how much they end up achieving. So how can you get out of this claustrophobia-inducing mindset and loosen up a bit for your own good?

Be Kind to Yourself: Being kind to ourselves may be easy on some days - when we are on a temporary self-esteem high, or simply are having a good day. But then, suddenly, we make a mistake, or are made aware of a weakness or setback. Our inner voice becomes an inner critic, and we somehow forget all the things that we previously were proud of ourselves for. We abandon ourselves and look towards others for validation and comfort.

Self-kindness refers to acting in kind and understanding ways towards ourselves. For instance, showing forgiveness and understanding for the mistakes we make - just as we show (hopefully!) to those around us. Humanity is blessed with the recognition that everyone makes mistakes sometimes, and no one is exempt from weaknesses or occasional failures. Extensive research has shown the copious positive consequences of self-compassion for overall wellbeing - including greater life satisfaction, emotional intelligence, connections and relationships with others, wisdom, and happiness. Self-compassion is also associated with fewer instances of depression, anxiety, fear of failure, and of course - perfectionism.

**Lower Your Standards**: You might not like the sound of this one, but hear me out! One of the most toxic elements of perfectionism is the tendency to set unrealistic goals and standards. For instance, you may decide you want to finish writing your novel in two weeks, and then berate yourself when the time window you set for yourself passes, and you don't manage. Or you may decide that you need to get 100% in all of your exams in order to feel like you did yourself proud. But this is a near-impossible feat, even for the most intellectual and conscientious of students - and getting around 80-90% in each test may be more than enough, as well as a clear indication of your excellence. So why set unachievable standards that only serve to give you a sense of disappointment even when in reality, your achievements may be truly great. The simple belief that 'if I don't meet this particular standard, then I am a failure' is toxically perfectionistic. There is no allowance for a middle ground. No flexibility in terms of what could be deemed a successful outcome. It is either success or failure, and that's that. But this isn't how life works!

In fact, it's possible to be just 80% or 75% successful - even a 30% success does not equate to failure. You may not have ticked all the boxes this time - but some of them, you did. And next time you will tackle the rest. So snap out of the black-and-white way of thinking that makes you believe every outcome only has two options - good or bad, yes or no, pass or fail. Open yourself up to nuance and the scope for possibility multiplies. Suddenly, it's not all about winning or losing anymore. It's about how you succeed, and how you learn from the times when you don't. It's about striving for excellence in all that you do, part of which is the learning process that lies behind every mistake. In that sense, failure is little more than feedback. And we all need feedback in order to better ourselves!

Another common perfectionist mindset is that 'if I am not the absolute best, then I'm no good at all.' This toxically competitive mindset is based on the idea that perfect means first place - and anything less equates to failure. This black-and-white approach to your achievements is not only blinkered to the many possible outcomes other than "first" or "last" - or "perfect" and "imperfect" - but it is also far too heavily focused on external measures. Essentially, you are comparing your own success to others' rather than focusing on your own unique journey. Many of us find this attitude hard to shake off after a decade or two of an education system ingraining within us the idea of grades and rankings - making us obsessed with the details, and comparing ourselves to our peers. But out in the real world, it doesn't have to be this way!

So, how to overcome this lingering grade-A student attitude?

**Set Time Limits**: One thing that your perfectionist attitude will never be able to overcome, despite its best efforts, is time. By setting hard time limits for projects and sticking to them, you will force yourself to come to draw lines under your endeavors before they manage to send you spiraling into hyper-vigilant perfectionist mode. Preening and re-doing your work obsessively when it was most likely already great before you started overthinking it will do you no favors. If you are naturally a perfectionist, you likely drive yourself mad by oscillating between wanting to always be on time, and wanting everything to be perfect. But not every task you do can take up huge amounts of your time and energy. It simply isn't feasible.

Of course, there are tasks that call for more of your attention than others, but if you find yourself going over and over every projects or endeavor, to the point that your eyes are sore and your brain feels about to explode by the time you press send or hand something in, it may be time for you to be stricter with yourself (dare I use such a word to a perfectionist!) when it comes to time. At some point, you must have a cut-off, where you lay that task to rest - at least for the time being. You may need to be more disciplined about when you leave the office for the day, or how long you spend on an assignment. It will feel unnatural at first to stop something before you would usually feel compelled to, but both your schedule and your mental health will thank you!

**Get used to making mistakes**: Ah, mistakes. Realistically, you won't exactly be welcoming them, but once they've already turned up unannounced, you may as well see what they have to say! Embracing that you will inevitably make mistakes and becoming more willing to learn from them is one of the most important things you can learn. However, perfectionists hate making mistakes. But because they don't allow themselves to make them, and when they do they refuse to learn anything from them as they are too busy punishing themselves, they may miss out on vital opportunities to learn and grow.

**Understand the real issue**: When most people "confess" to being a perfectionist, they wear it as some sort of badge of honor. The problem is, perfectionism is nothing more than a label we place on ourselves to hide the fact that we are deeply afraid of failure. Afraid of what others will think. Even, afraid of success. The last one sounds peculiar, but think about this - what does a perfectionist do once they have "made it"? Once they eventually achieve that near-impossible goal that they were living and breathing for? Do you think they basque in the exhilaration of it all? Unlikely. They usually immediately look towards the next milestone. And then the next, and the next. For a perfectionist, nothing is ever enough. And so, they live their lives in some sort of furlough between hurdles they set out for themselves, but never allowing themselves to celebrate each one as it is achieved.

If you worry that this is you, the easiest way to overcome fear is to face it head on. Don't obsess over what could happen, or how things might not work out - if you feel compelled to try, then go for it! Failure often isn't as painful as the anticipation of it - and the blow is softened by the satisfaction that you tried, and have now learned something about how to improve next time.

### The Bottom Line

As a society, we struggle to deal with the unusual and the unknown. We often choose to stick to a tried-and-tested formula, rather than take the risk and create a new one for ourselves. As a result, we favor those who stick to the rules rather than those bold enough to rewrite them - even if these are the people who end up being the most influential in the end. In this quest for familiarity, reassurance, and validation, we reject the slightest deviation from the paths we lay out for ourselves. Any unexpected result or setback, any mistake we make along the way, is interpreted as a disaster - rather than the natural bump in the road that it is.

Having unrealistic expectations about ourselves contributes to increased anxiety, depression, and general life dissatisfaction.

This self-targeting perfectionism is usually the result of trying to live up to a self-inflicted unrealistic ideal, but it can also be motivated by the fear of failure or judgment from others.

Of course, setting high standards for ourselves inspires us to do the very best that we can to achieve our potential and to approach life with motivation and ambition. As such, a certain level of perfectionism can be healthy in this regard, but when it becomes unhealthy and disruptive, it can cause serious problems both to mental health and to - ironically - your performance.

Extreme perfectionists tend to be overthinkers as they approach their life with an "all or nothing" mentality. But the world isn't all black and white! Most things in life, and most things you will do during your life, are not a binary in this way. Things don't tend to be simply "good" or" bad," as everything is filled with nuance and complexity. As such, if we live our life scrutinizing every shade of grey and categorizing it as either black or white, not only is this an utter waste of time and mental energy, but we will drive ourselves mad in the process.

Managing perfectionism often requires changing the way you perceive life - both success and failure. Just because things don't go 100% as you planned them, or if things didn't go exactly as you wanted, doesn't mean that you should write it off as a failure. Rather, see what did go right and acknowledge what you learned from the experience. Learn to be able to walk away from something that you don't deem "perfect" and feel at ease, realizing that perfection isn't natural, and often not even desirable. We're all just winging things as we go along, after all! Excellence, on the other hand, encourages this drive and ambition, and yet leaves room for the mistakes you will make, the deviations in the road, and acknowledges the full scope that "success" can truly mean.

# Chapter 6

## Indecisiveness and how to fight it

One of the key occasions where we tend to overthink is when it comes to making decisions - however big or small. Many people who have a tendency to overthink make the mistake of trying to predict all possible scenarios and only end up getting stuck by ending up deliberating over it so much that they lose clarity.

When you're not confident about a decision you're making, it's tempting to just avoid it altogether. Perhaps you've become indecisive due to a specific trauma, insecurity, or distraction. Alternatively, maybe you've simply always lived in fear of making the "wrong" choice or doing the "wrong" thing. Regardless of the root cause of your indecisiveness, it likely leaves you feeling frustrated and even powerless. But what can you do to take ownership of your freedom to choose, and stop being so indecisive?

Overthinkers tend to struggle to make decisions because they don't have enough faith in their ability to think for themselves; they believe that other people are more capable than themselves when it comes to making the "right" choice. In this scenario, you may feel compelled to always consult others who you trust more than yourself, in order to feel more confident in their decisions. The problem here is that this gives other people control, when sometimes you simply have to make your own choices, free from the influences of others. This is for your own good - for your self-esteem just as much as for your sense of autonomy. If you continuously hand over responsibility for your own decisions to others, you forfeit your own control and authority. You must learn to trust yourself by cultivating adequate self-belief and self-confidence. No one else can replace your own authority in your life. Some things, you must learn to do for yourself.

One way to beat overthinking is to beat indecision. To take control of your choices rather than handing them over to others. This will give you a sense of increased confidence and clarity when it comes to taking action in your life.

# Why do you struggle so much to make decisions?

*The curse of indecisiveness*

But why is it that some people seem to struggle to make even the smallest decisions - such as which shampoo to buy or what to make for dinner? Health and Wellness Expert, Caleb Backe, stated the following:

"Some people can't/don't make decisions because they are too busy over-analyzing everything. They analyze things to death, and are satisfied with that. They justify to themselves that they are not ignoring the problems. Quite the opposite — they are always thinking about them. But while thought is a wonderful thing, it is best coupled with an action. That jump from theoretical to practical is one which has a strong element of risk and danger in it. Some thrive on that feeling, but most of us are not ready to deal with it in many areas of our life."

If you are a member of this over-analyzing, overthinking, indecisive club, then fear not. You at least can never be accused of running away from your problems! However, as with most things, balance is key. Just as you shouldn't avoid thinking about important things in your life, you also shouldn't become consumed by every

single decision you have to make. It's estimated that the average adult makes about 35,000 remotely conscious decisions each day. Granted - some of these even overthinkers will make almost on

instinct - such as whether to smile at a stranger, or whether you walk around or straight through a puddle in your path - but can you even imagine how much time and mental energy you could save by not agonizing over even just half of these decisions?

# Decision Fatigue explained

*How even the smallest decisions can be draining your mental energy*

Research into the psychology of indecisiveness reveals a whole host of negative repercussions, with it limiting your success in everything; from your career to your personal relationships. Furthermore, there appear to be diverse causes of this struggle. As such, whatever causes indecisiveness in you may not be the same thing that provokes it in someone else. However, there are certain key sources to look for that that commonly impact one's ability to independently make decisions:

**Living to Please**

The core of your indecisiveness may lie in trying too hard to please other people. You might think that if you sit back and let others get their own way, then you'll get more approval, and external validation. As already discussed, depending too heavily on the opinions of others for your own sense of self-worth and direction is inherently harmful and takes away your own sense of self and autonomy. Essentially, if you get into the habit of letting everyone else go before you while you remain passive when it comes to making a decision, your self-belief and ability to make your own choices only further weakens with time.

**Broken Self-Trust**

Alternatively, after a procession of bad choices or simply negative outcomes that you blame on your own decisions, you may lose faith in your own judgment as a consequence. A lack of self-belief and self-trust can be debilitating, as you know longer allow yourself to have any sort of authority on decisions - big or small.

It may be that you made one too many work mistakes for you to feel you can forgive yourself, or maybe whatever you wear leaves you feeling embarrassed.

**Paralysis of Choice**

And then there's the concept of choice-paralysis, coined by French philosophers in the 20th century. The idea is that we are faced with so many choices in the developed world today - more so now than ever before - that we can actually feel paralyzed as a result - unable to choose just one of the many options. Whether it's the endless brands of the same simple product at the supermarket, the endless career or studying opportunities that lie before you, or the unfathomable amount of potential people to seek a relationship with thanks to the internet connecting us to more people than ever before - it can be overwhelming to even think about choosing just one anything. Working out how to make up your mind can be that much harder when you're literally spoilt for choice.

# The 40/70 Rule of Decision-Making
*The ultimate trick to stop overthinking your decisions*

An excellent approach to consider to beat your indecisiveness is Colin Powell's 40/70 rule. Once we have established whether we have gathered the information necessary to make an informed choice, we then - in theory - use our instincts to avoid thinking about it too much. Our ability to become successful marketers, leaders, managers, or entrepreneurs depends upon this crucial ability to make informed and yet not over-thought choices on a constant basis.

From designing a new product to making a bold business or strategic move, most career paths are rife with continuous decisions. On top of that, the outcomes can have huge effects down the line, only adding to the pressure of our choices. And just as some thrive on the sense of power provided by this, for others, it can send your head into a spin, as every step you take, you feel the need to look closely at the ground before gingerly placing your foot… Research has proven that the best leaders are those who have the ability to make important decisions, both thoughtfully and confidently. The point is: anybody can make "snap decisions" -and these aren't often advised - however, to do so both quickly and effectively is the hack we all need.

## Enter: The 40/70 rule

Here's the thing: every single choice that you make is composed of a range of elements - such as your own self-confidence, your understanding of the issue at hand, your experience in the subject, and your determination to be proactive and take action. The threshold for all of these components to come together and assist in the arrival at a definitive decision is where things can get a little more complicated…

The previous US Secretary of State, Colin Powell, came up with something called the 40/70 rule. The idea behind it is that when you have between 40 and 70% of the details needed to make a decision, this is when you are best equipped to make a choice. No more, no less.

Try to make a decision with less than 40% of the information, and you're stabbing in the dark. But wait until you have more than 70% of the info, and you find that you actually waited for too long, and may now end up being overwhelmed which leads to indecisiveness.

The 40/70 rule comes in two parts in its approach to decision-making. Powell specifies that you do require a sufficient level of information in order to make an informed choice on the matter - but not so much that you run the risk-taking too long or beating around the bush, hesitating before you take the necessary action.

## Part I: Determine Your Information Percentage

To get a better understanding of where exactly you fall into this elusive 40-70 range, Powell presents the following formula:

P = 40 to 70

Here, P equates to the likelihood of success, and the numbers indicate the portion of information that you have. While a definitive percentage can be hard to come up with, you need to approximate where you believe you fall within this window, based on exactly what details you have.

## Part II: Trust Your Instincts

After you've reached that sweet spot between 40 and 70 percent, it's then up to your instincts to make the final decision. This part is what distinguishes the leaders from the crowd, because it's not exclusively about the facts - but also involves your intrinsic impulse - and of course, your trust in it.

## The Consequences of your Actions

Since there are consequences for every action, there are also long-reaching after-effects for inaction. This notion is what determines the minimum amount of information to make a choice, according to the 40-70 rule.

Making a decision when you have less than 40% of the information needed can result in a failure to acknowledge particular elements of the issue can lead you to make decisions that don't fully address the circumstances. On top of that, ill-informed choices can inflict unfavorable implications for either yourself, your project, or other people involved in this choice. And finally, you risk making an objectively incorrect decision that could have been avoided had you gotten more details before making it.

On the other hand, making a decision when you have more than 70% of the details needed can result in you overthinking every minute aspect of the issue, causing you to become lost in the details, and blind to the bigger picture. You may also experience this aforementioned phenomenon of choice paralysis, now that you are so immersed in all the different options and what they could mean, there is no one particular option that stands out to you. And so you continue to overthink, to deliberate, and things only decrease in clarity. You may never even manage to make a decision in the end as it all becomes too much! Or, you get so frustrated that you end up choosing one opinion on a whim, just so that the turmoil will end - and this only results in the same negative consequences of making an uninformed choice, as listed above.

So next time you're confronted with a predicament that requires a definitive answer, try approaching it with the 40/70 rule in mind, making sure that you're setting yourself up for the best possible outcomes. Of course, you're not always going to make the ideal call - as i hope you will remember from the last chapter, such perfection is not even possible! However, by using this formula combined with your gut instinct, you're most likely to maintain a constant, robust, and yet efficient decision-making process.

# How to beat indecision
*How to stop every decision being a huge affair.*

What are some more concrete steps you can take from today to help your frazzled, decision-fatigued mind, and clear up a little more space for the important stuff? Here are some interesting tactics you could consider:

**Don't sweat the small stuff**

Do you know what Barack Obama and Mark Zuckerberg have in common (besides being American, and high achievers that is)? They both have been known to wear pretty much the exact same thing every single day: Obama sports a dark blue suit, and Zuckerberg a grey tee-shirt. And they do this for the same intriguing reason: to spare their overworked minds of one less little decision each day.

As discussed previously, we only have a limited amount of mental energy in a given day - and this, of course, still applies if you're the former leader of the free world or the founder of one of the world's most well-known companies!

You have probably experienced yourself when you simply can't form an opinion anymore. Often, it's the small stuff that won't inflict drastic consequences either way – what to have for breakfast, what film to watch, or indeed – what clothes to put on each day. We all have so much else going on in our overworked brains that we can end up hitting a wall when presented with a less important decision that we have no strong opinion about either way. It's as though our minds have given up – they may jump into gear if suddenly presented with an emergency or pressing matter – but sometimes it's the trivial stuff that we struggle with the most. Psychologists call this phenomenon "decision fatigue."

Roy F. Baumeister, a psychologist specialized in decision fatigue, told the New York Times:

'Making decisions uses the very same willpower that you use to say no to doughnuts, drugs, or illicit sex. It's the same willpower that you use to be polite or to wait your turn or to drag yourself out of bed or to hold off going to the bathroom. Your ability to make the right investment or hiring decision may be reduced simply because you expended some of your willpower earlier when you held your tongue in response to someone's offensive remark or when you exerted yourself to get to the meeting on time.'

And as Obama notoriously confessed to Vanity Fair back in 2012 while he was still in office, surviving as a key political figure without your brain exploding requires that you throw out the more mundane decisions such as deciding what to wear, or what to have for breakfast – which others may cloud their minds with – every single morning. He stated:

'You'll see I wear only grey or blue suits. I'm trying to pare down decisions. I don't want to make decisions about what I'm eating or wearing. Because I have too many other decisions to make.'

Facebook founder, Mark Zuckerberg had a similar take, stating: 'I really want to clear my life to make it so that I have to make it so that I have to make as few decisions as possible about anything except how to best serve this community.'

Okay, I'm not suggesting we all go around wearing the same thing every single day so that everywhere looks like a dystopian "Black Mirror" episode and self-expression and creativity become a crime. This technique works more for some than for others. And if you get a great deal of joy and self-expression out of what you wear, then you do you! But I encourage you to distinguish important decisions from more minor ones. Prioritize where you spend your mental energy. This is done with the aim of not occupying our whole mind for less important choices - for example, giving ourselves short time for small decisions, or limiting the options we have - in order to provide more time to the most critical decisions that require more rigorous reflection. I must reiterate the benefit of putting a deadline on our decisions to avoid constant overthinking. Start by setting short time-limits for small decisions, as well as some sort of deadline, even for bigger decisions.

## Tune Into Your Emotions

As an overthinking and indecisive person, one of the first things you must try to do is to stop over-analyzing. Easier said than done, I know. This tendency comes from the fact you don't trust your instincts, which, as I mentioned earlier, is a vital part of becoming empowered. Consequently, if you work on more deeply tuning into your emotions, you'll develop your intrinsic finely honed intuitions (yes, we all have them, but many of us forget!) that help you confidently make choices without over-analyzing.

Whether you want to learn how to stop being indecisive in your relationships with others, or are thinking more about your career or wider life choices, being more emotionally aware can help in all of these areas. You must ask whether your hesitation is due to a deep fear of not being prepared or capable enough, or an anxiety of what could happen if you make the wrong choice - causing you to shake under the weight of all the potential outcomes - good and bad.

If it's fear of incapacity, simply proceed with one manageable step at a time. Learn from each one and keep moving forward. Your confidence and self-belief will solidify as you go on, making it easier and easier to trust yourself and take action each time. If it's anxiety of the unknown, then jump right in - put yourself in a position where you don't have the luxury of time to overthink. It seems harsh, but it may be the only way to kickstart yourself into action and break the habit of senseless rumination. So make a commitment you can't back down from. Accept your anxiety as something that will come and go, and power through anyway.

Of course, this may sound good in theory, but how do you reliably put it into practice? Try proving the worth of your intuitions by making a list of five times in life when your gut instinct was right. Maybe it was your first impressions of an individual who has since made an impact in your life. Or maybe it was a work decision or an important lifestyle change that ended up working out for the best in the long-run. Whatever it is, cultivate a broader self-awareness by keeping a daily journal and reflecting on your emotions, your gut feelings, and your predictions. Even just a few minutes spent doing this each day can help you vastly by tapping into those reflective and intuitive capacities that have long been dormant or ignored.

## Learn To Trust Yourself

Overcoming indecisiveness is also about finding your unique strengths and figuring out how you can apply them to help your decision-making process.

If you're like most of my clients who struggle with indecision, you might find it difficult to pinpoint your strengths. After all, this in itself requires a certain level of confidence and self-awareness that indecisive individuals often lack in the first place. But trust me - even if it isn't clear, I am certain that you have many useful and applicable personal strengths. And it's about time you harnessed their potential!

Try to list at least five of your main strengths. Think of the strengths others have acknowledged in you. Are you well-organized, a very personable individual, or maybe you have a particular way with numbers or with words? Perhaps you're known for your unique sense of humor or your unfailing optimism in times of difficulty. Take your time to really think it through - reflecting on your past achievements, experiences, and interactions with others.

Next, think of at least one way that each of these specific strengths could be used to facilitate your decision-making. For example, optimism can be used to increase your confidence of making a choice by reminding you that you can survive any outcome of the decision, anyway. Meanwhile, your interpersonal skills may mean that you can talk your way out of any situation, or always rely on communicating with others to receive support if things don't go to plan.

## Visualize All Possible Outcomes

When figuring out how to make difficult life decisions, although too much can be risky for overthinkers, visualization takes you closer to the reality of the different options. This can then make the right choice for you become much clearer and offer some much-needed reassurance that a decision isn't as foreboding as you feared. If you already have some experience with visualization - for example, via mindfulness meditation, as I will get into more deeply later in this book - you'll find that this technique comes pretty naturally.

That being said, even if you're totally new to visualization and aren't really sure what I mean by it, you can pick it up quickly. Simply close your eyes and breathe deeply until you feel relaxed. Allow yourself to detach slightly from your reality - all preconceived biases and ideas. All worries about what others may decide, or what you feel you should decide. Just focus on you and your own gut feeling. Then, use your imagination to hypothetically embed yourself in all the possible choices before you. Notice how you feel in each scenario. Which one feels the most natural, or that puts you most at ease? Trust your instinct to guide you to the right one.

If this kind of creative visualization really doesn't work for you or just sounds a bit abstract, there are other approaches you may prefer. For instance, try drawing up a mind map as another way of visualizing your options, but in a more linear and logical way for those who are more that way inclined. But be careful that this strategy doesn't veer off into over-analysis...

## Take Your Own Sweet Time

While I have already laid our reasons why you should sometimes set time limits when making decisions, there are some cases where taking your time is preferable. For instance, new psychological research reveals that if you take a short break from thinking about a choice, you often end up making a better thought-out decision. This links to what I pointed out earlier about changing up your environment in order to feed creativity and mental clarity. The same applies here.

The issue is that we can sometimes become entrapped by paranoia about making a decision under time pressure, and this can create additional anxiety. The anxiety, and the brain fog and panic implicated, then makes it almost impossible to single out one choice. When you feel that this might be happening to you, put the decision aside for a while. Allow your mind to wander onto other things as you focus on something else for a while, take a short break or a quick walk. See how much more clear-minded and calm you feel once you return to thinking about the decision.

## Take Action

When overcoming a history or simply a bout of indecisiveness, it's important to remember that you can learn from both your successes, and from your mistakes. In other words - even if you mess up and make the "wrong" choice from time to time, remember that you're human and not a machine. Buckle up and try it again. You will develop both your experience and your confidence with time, regardless of the mistakes you make along the way.

Learning what works for you, personally, is a process of trial and error in itself, that relies on your own willingness to put yourself out there and experiment. It's only when you attempt different techniques, like the ones discussed above, that you'll actually be able to determine what will push you towards better and more effective decision-making.

Additionally, try to make a habit of willingly stepping outside of your comfort zone. Step up and take action in every area of your life, rather than exclusively the areas you feel particularly comfortable with. And do this while bearing in mind that you can make something good away from every possible result - whether or not things go as you planned, as long as you open yourself up to new opportunities for learning and growing. When you see things this way, it's a win-win! You either succeed, or you learn how to better succeed next time. Because, even when things don't turn out as you'd expected or would have liked, this is what provides the most fertile soil for healthy growth. In truth, it is often those lessons we learn from our most gut-wrenching mistakes that lead us to something better in the future. So slowly allow yourself to become more at ease and accustomed to putting yourself out there - stepping up to new challenges, trying new things, and pushing your self-imposed limits. If you want something in your life to change, the first change starts with your own actions, after all. Feeding your own resilience, adaptability, and versatility in this way is one of the most effective ways to prove to yourself that you have the power to own your decisions and handle whatever comes your way as a result of them.

### The Bottom Line

I should probably finish by pointing out that indecision isn't always bad. Sometimes, hesitation before making a choice gives you valuable time to think about the whole situation. If you can't seem to arrive at an answer quickly, it may just be a sign that what's at stake really matters to you, and you rightfully don't want to mess up. This need for extended thought and reflection is, of course, necessary from time to time. The most important thing is to not let indecision keep you stuck forever. Deliberate when you need to, but you have to make a choice eventually. And although some decisions may take more time and analysis than others, don't allow yourself to become completely paralyzed every time you are presented with a fork in your path.

Make no mistake: Indecision becomes a disruptive thing when it lasts for too long. How long is too long, you may ask? Well, that depends on the specific context and circumstances. Will you miss an important opportunity by waiting? Could you lose something potentially very valuable just because of your hesitation? Is the decision getting harder or easier to make, the more time and energy you spend dwelling on it?

On top of that, indecision can sometimes become a decision by default. For instance, if you decide not to decide, you essentially forfeit your power of choice. Someone else might get chosen for that opportunity you spent so long mulling over, or another buyer might snap up that property you couldn't make your mind up about, but may have actually been your dream home.

Only you hold the keys to changing your mindset; Perhaps you have already labeled yourself an "indecisive person," but don't let this define you. You may have moments of indecisiveness or hesitance, but that's a habit you can overcome, not a personality trait! You can learn to make decisions, just like you learned to read or ride a bike. It's just a skill like any other.

If you don't start to take initiative within your own life, you'll only end up becoming a prisoner of your own indecisiveness. You'll limit your opportunities, not allowing yourself to be open to changes that could enhance your life and pave the way towards you achieving your goals and aspirations. To finish with a quote by Denis Waitley:

'Life is inherently risky. There is only one big risk you should avoid at all costs, and that is the risk of doing nothing.'

# Chapter 7

## Procrastination cure

We all procrastinate from time to time - "I'll do it later" or "I can't start until I do x, y, and z," - but most of us don't really consider the reasons why we do this, or consider that it can actually be linked to anxiety and overthinking - rather than just laziness.

Overthinking, unfortunately, has a close link with low productivity. We often postpone tasks to be carried out until we really cannot put it off anymore, although knowing that these are important and should be carried out immediately. This behavior is due primarily to factors such as fear of failure, perfectionism, and incorrect organization of the task and thoughts - but it actually only increases your anxiety and fear of failure, as you end up having to rush something at the last minute and when under duress, rather than taking your time so that you can produce your best word.

# Am I just a lazy bastard?

*The difference between laziness and executive*

I will get into some of the common reasons beyond procrastination later on, but first of us, we need to rule out one thing. Are you just being lazy? Is there a deeper reason for your putting off of this task, or is this all it boils down to. Essentially, are you experiencing an executive function (a non-deliberate failure to do things on time), or an executive dysfunction (a deliberate "putting things off until later" situation)?

Let me explain a little better.

Executive function is the process of identifying, planning, executing, and following through with tasks. And so, if you have a dysfunction regarding any of these components - that would imply an executive dysfunction. This implies that rather than being a procrastinator, there is actually another underlying cause.

For instance, it could be that you have an issue with figuring out what needs to be done or where to even begin. You may have difficulty managing your time, and so can't map out a time when exactly you can do something. Lastly, you may simply be disorganized - perhaps because your brain is so cluttered with your overthinking habit - that you struggle to even remember the tasks you need to do. You end up frazzled and having to catch up, or feel overwhelmed and simply feel unable to face the task once you remember that it exists.

All of this, as well as countless other scenarios, are examples of executive dysfunction. There is some part of your productivity chain that is lacking, and this is why your work isn't getting done as it should be.

Procrastination, on the other hand, is a deliberate choice. This is when you have an executive function but are not getting your tasks done because you are putting them off. You don't want to do your assignment, go to the gym, or read that report, so you don't. Of course, even this isn't simple. You may truly want to do these things deep down for the long-term benefits you would reap - you know it's the right thing to do - but something is stopping you. At the end of the day, it is still a conscious choice not to do it - but there could be an unconscious reason behind this choice.

# The Roots of Procrastination
*Why do you really put off the work you need to do?*

As mentioned, procrastination is a conscious decision to put something off until later, to prioritize your short-term comfort for your long-term gain. Now, this could be just because you really don't want to do the task at hand - or, for no other reason than that, it's hard and you can't be bothered. However, what many people don't realize is that there is often an underlying root to your procrastination in any one instance - even if you are not conscious of it at the time. The most likely sources of your procrastination are fear, disorganization, and perfectionism, which can then be further divided into several principal causes.

They go as follows:

## Procrastination due to your memory being overwhelmed

For example, you get overwhelmed by all the tasks firing your way at work. There seem to be so many things that you need to do, that you can hardly manage to focus on just one. This links to what I discussed in an earlier chapter about sticking to one task until it's complete, and not falling for the myth of multitasking. But sometimes, when you feel like you're completely swimming in requests and demands, this is quite the exercise for your mental concentration and certainly easier said than done...

If you're anything like my clients, even noting things down on a calendar or diary can feel overwhelming, as you end up with a messy visualization of all the chaos in your mind. The solution to this is to find a way to schedule your time, separate chunks of your time to concentrate wholly on specific tasks, so your mind doesn't become overcrowded, and to find a way to remind yourself only once it becomes necessary of the next oncoming task. Electronic calendar alerts or project management tools are great for this, as it will only show specific alerts when you actually need to see them.

## Procrastination due to fear of the unknown

Fear of uncertainty or anything unfamiliar is another common cause of anxiety problems which can also feed into your procrastination habit. Do you have a general tendency to feel stuck whenever you feel uncertain about doing something? Or perhaps you obsess over where to start to such a point that you become fearful to even approach the task?

Similarly, do you tend to overthink every possible scenario before you take that first step? If this is the case, you run the risk of getting caught up in details rather than grasping the big picture.

## Procrastination due to unrealistic standards and expectations

As touched upon earlier, black-and-white, all-or-nothing thinking is a surefire way to leave you battling anxiety and overthinking. But how can this lead you to procrastinate? Could you save yourself some unnecessary stress by doing a task you've been avoiding, yet in a way more in line with where you feel comfortable and like you can perform your best? For instance, could you break it into small chunks rather than attempting the whole thing at once?

Or maybe there's a way you can put your own spin on the task, to make it somehow more "your own" - which can not only allow you to tap into your flow state but will likely result in a much more passion-fed and therefore high-quality result. Obviously, there's not always much room for adaptation, depending on the task. But there often is more flexibility than you may have been thinking - and a way to make the task seem less daunting.

Sometimes it's not an all-or-nothing scenario - you can complete a task yet in a more creative, or at least in a more comfortable way. To give this a go in a more relatable sense, try to identify just one task that you're dreading that you'd be less likely to avoid if you reduced your or changed your standards - as well as what kinds of standards you can realistically afford to adapt.

## Procrastination due to negative assumptions

It's often the case that when someone drags their heels on a task, it's quite simply because they're predicting a negative outcome. If you have already convinced yourself that something won't work, or will end in failure, then it makes you less enthusiastic about attempting it. Your subconscious is simply trying to spare you the trouble! But the catch is that we often get it wrong - we can't always predict what an outcome will be. I'm sure you can recall times where you were sure something would fail, only to be

pleasantly surprised. Well, imagine if you never even tried? You would still be convincing yourself that it wasn' with attempting.

The truth is, half the battle is noticing that you're making a negative prediction - as it can often be unconscious Recognise first of all, as I discuss at length (especially in my last book on self-confidence!) that failure is not your enemy anyway. It can be your best teacher. But also realize that a negative outcome is only one of the possible outcomes. Try the three questions technique, where you identify three potential outcomes: the worst, the best, and finally - the most realistic. By imagining the worst and best-case scenarios first, you will be better able to determine the most likely outcome - that almost always comes somewhere in the middle, and isn't as bad as you'd feared.

**Procrastination due to lack of drive**

This is another topic I discussed at length in my last book on self-confidence. One key component of your self-belief - that often goes overlooked, even within positive psychology "self-development" circles, is self-efficacy. In case you aren't;t familiar with this term, self-efficacy refers to your drive. You may be a confident person who still is lacking in this department. That's because self-efficacy is focused on your actions rather than your thoughts or intentions. For instance, someone who talks themselves up gloats about the businesses they will start, the places they will travel to, or the goals they have maybe a self-confident person with some big aspirations. However, it is self-efficacy that actually makes you get up and do those things. To make your dreams a reality outside of your own head...

And so, if you feel this may be what you are lacking, then know that you are already halfway there! If you're the type to make big plans but not always follow them through, then first recognize that the fact that you have big plans and know what you want to do is already a great step. Next, focus on what exactly is preventing you from actually taking the leap to get the ball rolling on these big plans... The next section may help you with this.

## The Types of Procrastination

So you now know whether you have a procrastination rather than simply an executive dysfunction problem. And if the former, you may have even determined the main source of your procrastination. But this isn't the full story.

How does your procrastination manifest? That's what we will delve into next:

### Anxious-Perfectionist Procrastinator

As an overthinker, it's pretty likely that your procrastination is laced with anxiety. This could either stem from your perfectionism, as already discussed, making you put off tasks until you have perfect conditions, perfect background knowledge, or won't submit something until it meets your unrealistically perfect expectations. Although many may believe that these perfectionist types are more productive than most, it can actually hinder your productivity, as you may delay processes and not actually complete things on time as they never seem to be good enough for you.

Stanford University Philosopher, John Perry, proposes that procrastinating can actually be a good thing for perfectionists...

'As long as they have a lot of time to do a task, they fantasize about doing a perfect job. Leaving it till the last minute is a way of giving oneself permission to do a merely adequate job. 99% of the time, a merely adequate job is all that is needed.'

Try looking back at the last five tasks you completed. Were they all perfect, honestly? Were they good enough, though? The chances are, if you have overthinking and perfectionist tendencies, that you're already working to a high standard even when you don't think you are - so stop giving yourself such a hard time!

Identifying those times where you didn't do such a perfect job, but the consequences were just the same as though you had, will help you to overcome your perfectionist routine and stop procrastinating. Sometimes good is good enough!

## Exhausted Procrastinator

Another common type of procrastination is simply down to your own well-being. This often goes hand-in-hand with anxiety-fuelled procrastination. It basically means you are so overworked or overburdened, that you are not physically or mentally your best. You may be sleep-deprived, malnourished, dehydrated, or simply starved of downtime. Whatever it is, how can you expect to perform your best when your most basic needs are not met? If you procrastinate, you may feel guilty about downtime as you are plagued with thoughts of all the things you really ought to be doing. But without adequate rest, we can't achieve anything. We are not machines!

And so, to overcome this type of procrastination, you may need to actually incorporate downtime into your busy schedule. It could be "social media time," "call-a-friend time," "read a chapter time," or even "Netflix time"! Whatever you need to unwind and feel ready for the next onslaught of work. It isn't anything to feel guilty about. And once it is officially incorporated into your schedule, you won't feel so deprived during your actual working time. Like a kid, don't deprive them of fun, and they will likely behave a lot better!

## Fun-Seeking Procrastinator

On the reverse side, and yet still on a related note, the fun-seeking procrastinator would rather be doing literally anything except that one dreaded task that they're supposed to be working on. And the more they think about what they should be doing, the more impossible it becomes to drag themselves away from their preferred pastime... Now, if there's simply no way that you're ever going to start on that one so-dreaded task, at the very least, have a go at indulging in some more structured procrastination. This may not be what you expected - but if you're going to procrastinate anyway, why not make it on your own terms? Allow yourself to procrastinate a little and on your terms (see above), but once your fun-time is over and you still can't focus, then start another item on your to-do list.

Often, by avoiding this particular task - even if you are only replacing it with another -, you get that same sense of satisfaction and may even come back to it feeling more able, having managed to tick off something else on your list. Procrastination and productivity in one, I hear you say? Double win.

**Directionless Procrastinator**

Most people find it to be an uphill struggle to start a project when the deadline seems like it is a long way off. There's an absence of a sense of urgency or immediate obligation that many of us require to jump into action. Indeed, sometimes a little pressure is actually good for us as it keeps us moving forward without too much dilly-dallying. And then there are those tasks you know need to get done, but that don't have a deadline at all - which can be especially hard to get down to.

To overcome this "lost" feeling when there is a loose or non-existent lime limit, try setting your own deadlines and noting them down - even saying them aloud either to someone else (who will listen!) or simply to yourself. This active commitment and the associated sense of obligation that comes along with it may actually be all it takes to keep you on track and motivate you to keep your head in the game until you meet those deadlines you set for yourself.

# Sabotaging your Self-sabotaging behaviours

*Are you self-sabotaging without realising it?*

Have you ever found that things are going well for you - either in your career, your relationship, or perhaps just your overall contentment - only for you to do something inexplicable that damages the success you're reaping and forces you back a few steps? You stop putting the effort in at work, or blow up with your partner or loved one for no good reason? Or, maybe you mentally berate yourself when you're in the midst of an important challenge. This could make you feel increasingly discouraged and frustrated, and angry at yourself, which prevents you from reaching your potential, achieving the desired mental state of "flow," and doing whatever it is that you need to do for your own self-development and success. All of these behaviors indicate that you may be unknowingly self-sabotaging.

Worrying, I know - aren't we supposed to be on our own side? The subconscious mind is cruel like that.

Sabotage is defined as 'the act of destroying or undermining something.' The term self-sabotage, then, is used when this destructive behavior is directed at yourself. Self-sabotage eats away at your self-confidence and self-esteem. And insidiously, with every failed attempt to complete a task or achieve something as you set out to, you unconsciously feel you have "proven" to yourself that you can't or shouldn't continue… You may not even be aware that you're doing this to yourself. However, when negative habits consistently throw your efforts off course - either at work or regarding your health and relationships - they can be considered a form of psychological self-harm.

Self-sabotage can manifest in many different behaviors, unique to each person. For instance, you might repeatedly "forget" your deadlines, or be consistently late to work. You may fail to prepare for a presentation or test adequately. In your personal life, you may keep making unhealthy choices you know you shouldn't, or push people away once they show affection for you.

Maybe you start projects but never finish them. You convince yourself, presented with an exciting opportunity, that you don't want to go for it, or that it's a stupid idea.

Self-sabotage is driven by self-destructive inner monologues. Basically, you tell yourself that you don't want something (when you do) or that you can't do something (when you can!). You find yourself thinking things like, "that's a stupid idea anyway," "is it really worth the effort?" or "why try?"

We've likely all acted out like this at some point. As I hope you will remember from the last chapter - perfection is a myth! However, some of us are more prone to self-sabotage than others, and the fact that it can be difficult to admit - even to ourselves - that we're doing it makes it even harder to identify and thus manage.

From my own experience, one of the main factors leading my clients' self-sabotage is a lack of self-esteem. Self-esteem and reasons why it may be low is a whole other issue (which you can find out more about in my last book on self-confidence if you haven't already!), but all you need to know in this context is that the effects of low self-esteem are largely predictable: feelings of worthlessness, the misled belief that you don't deserve happiness or success due to ruminating on past mistakes or negative feedback, and even a dangerous level of self-loathing. It's common among those with low self-esteem to worry that if they fail at something, their loved ones will think less of them - or that if they're successful, it won't last. And so, they act out to take control of what they deem the inevitable. To the subconscious mind, sabotaging your own happiness is better than someone else doing so...

In this way, self-sabotage is another kind of vicious cycle, as it reinforces this misplaced sense of worthlessness and inadequacy, and provides justification for negative thoughts that feed back into the behavior. It provides an escape route when things seem to be turning south - even if only in your mind. And if you are worried that something won't end well, it's a way of saying "look, I didn't want this anyway" to seemingly spare yourself the humiliation of seeming to care.

So, how to fix this? As you become more aware of the negative feelings, behaviors, and thought-processes that trigger your self-sabotage habit, you can begin to challenge them with more positive and more rational affirmations. Then, try to link this new positive inner monologue to what you can accomplish and what you truly want to achieve - your insecurities and fears set to one side. This can help to turn your irrational assumptions around and gain some much-needed perspective.

Tips or advice to facilitate your productivity are all well and good, but at the end of the day, action is what actually gets things done.

# Anti-procrastination techniques revealed
*How to beat the all-or-nothing mentality.*

For many, their procrastination stems from not caring enough. If you're not passionate about the work or feel that there is a greater purpose behind it that you find motivating, then it can be genuinely really difficult to apply yourself in spite of your daily distractions. As such, if procrastination is a persistent issue for you, consider if the underlying purpose - or lack thereof - of your work could be the reason.

Maybe, you're not lazy at all, or even particularly anxious. Rather, you are just looking for passion - and that's pretty commendable if you ask me! Just make sure you use this to your advantage and allow it to drive you to find a project or path that you can feel excited about.

That being said, sometimes you may actually have something to do that you simply must power through. We can't be excited all the time. That would make even excitement lose its excitement, I guess...

However, if your overall well-being and sense of purpose is in check, then those times where you have less enthralling, niggling tasks to complete won't seem so burdensome. You will be able to get your head down, get the work done, and come out of it feeling accomplished and ready to take on the tasks you find more enjoyable.

Laziness is different from procrastination - as it's possible to have one without the other. However, the same solutions for solving laziness can also be applied to procrastination in many cases. Here are five key tips for overcoming laziness-related

procrastination:

## Use the Two-minute Rule

Whenever you've got a task that you're thinking of putting off for later, ask yourself the following simple question: How long will this take? If the answer is two minutes or less, then do it straight away! This principle can also be applied to taller tasks because most tasks take less than two minutes to be set in motion - and then the rest will seem more achievable as you already made the first step.

## Start Immediately - Think Later

Often, we commit self-sabotage in the subtle way of doing other things before work. Of course,

starting is often the most dreaded part -  especially if you're dealing with chronic laziness or procrastination. So I say just start.

You can actually trick your mind to starting work. Try telling yourself that you'll only spend the first five minutes or so working before doing that other thing that's luring you away - like checking your social media or making coffee. The chances are that once you're already stuck in and on a roll, you'll realize that those things can wait.

## Ignore Your Distractions

In most situations, you can't avoid distractions, but you can ignore them if you really want to. For instance, if your co-workers discuss what happened at the bar last night, your friend is texting you about their love life, simply block out these distractions - you can engage later once your important work is done!

You can also block out certain notifications or put your phone on flight-mode if this is an easier way for you to remain focused. Just realize that most distractions can actually be muted if you truly want to - but that's another matter altogether!

The Bottom Line: Time To Be On Your Own Side!

This may not be something you want to hear, but the main cure to procrastination and laziness is taking action. So while the above-mentioned tips will work for some people, it may not work for others.

If you've tried a lot of things mentioned above - from setting calendar alerts, to taking scheduled breaks, to muting your social media, and are still having difficulties, then perhaps you just need to make an honest decision to start taking action on the things that matter to you.

However, once you are aware of the causes, the types, and the different possible manifestations of procrastination, as well as its link to self-sabotage, you are on the right track towards getting a handle on your own actions and productivity. Allowing yourself to take breaks or to reduce your expectations when necessary, but still being able to push yourself and learn to prioritize your time and mental energy to make your goals a reality, rather than floating dreams in your head! This way, you can fight your own corner, and be your own greatest coach and motivator - keeping any self-sabotaging behaviors at bay.

# Stop! Stop! Stop!

Here I am again to interrupt your reading!
I just wanted to check how the book was going, but if you got this far, I would say not so bad!
Would you like to let me know your thoughts by leaving a short review on amazon?
It shouldn't take you too much of your time, but I assure you it would be an invaluable gift for a small writer like me.

Scan here for
leaving a review!

I thank you in advance!

# Chapter 8

## Mindfulness meditation

A great and effective way to relieve excessive overthinking is to do meditation and mindfulness exercises. This allows you to release any nervous tension accumulated during working hours or moments of high mental or emotional effort or difficulty. Furthermore, during this physical and mental activity, we learn not to think, as we usually constantly do, but to instead seek this sought-after mental and emotional state of flow - neither over nor under-stimulated - that we have gone over previously.

If you're a natural overthinker, then there's always something whirring around your brain, spurring your fight-or-flight response in the process and making you feel perpetually on edge, constantly ready to jump into action - which isn't good for your peace - or your blood pressure! Mindfulness and meditation could be the final missing jigsaw piece you're subconsciously searching for to reconnect with yourself and free yourself from this heavy mental burden.

## Fix your body, fix your mind

*The power of breathing and rest for mental clarity.*

Meditation has blown up in the Western hemisphere during the past few years - from being almost solely associated with monks or hippies, to being a word that pops up daily as an inclusive practice that everyone is doing - or at the very least, thinking they ought to be doing!

But wait - don't write off meditation as dippy-hippy or reserved for California girls who go on Bali retreats. Meditation is beneficial for everyone and is actually much more straightforward and accessible once you see past all the "yogi" stereotypes of how you think someone who meditates should look or behave. There are actually many types of meditation and mindfulness exercises, as well as many medically proven neurological benefits (but more on that later…).

But what does true, neurologically nourishing, and non-performative meditation look like really? And how could it help you stop overthinking? Ray Dalio, American billionaire hedge fund manager, says the following regarding the impact of regular meditation on his life and success:

'When I look back at my life, I am happy to have had what most people would consider a successful life, not only regarding business but also in my relationships and in lots of ways. More than anything else, I attribute it to meditation—partially because of the creativity, partly because of the centeredness. TM has given me an ability to put things in perspective, which has helped a lot. I think meditation has been the single biggest influence on my life.'

In fact, many household names and leading CEOs attribute meditation and mindfulness to much of their success and ability to thrive - Oprah, Madonna, Arianna Huffington, and CEOs of LinkedIn (Jeff Weiner) and Ford Motors (Willian Clay) to name just a select few. Still need more convincing? How could meditation be incorporated into your own routine?

The main aim of meditation is to clear the mind and separate oneself from worldly or bodily distractions - from the mundane musings of what you're having for dinner or when your work is due, to the deeper stuff around your life's purpose or mistakes - meditation allows your mind a much-needed break that it seldom can't even get during sleep. This is traditionally supposed to enable you to reach a heightened level of awareness and inner peace. But now that the Buddhism-derived practice has become more mainstream even in western society, for many, it has become less of a spiritual practice, and more of a way to seek inner calm and a rest from the usual excessive thoughts. To reconnect with oneself and to attune oneself with the senses.

Overall, the ambiguity over the definition of meditation - with the focus more on the goal rather than the method - we are graciously left with a little wiggle room to tailor it to our own needs and preferences, making it work for us as we see fit. Of course, for some, this could well be preferable in the classic form of sitting in the lotus position with the palms facing upwards as they rest on the knees. However, for many, more creative exploration is required in order to truly sink into the intended restorative meditative state.

Perhaps the greatest appeal of meditation is that it is accessible to all, and requires no formal training or teacher. It's free, requires no fancy equipment or specific location - and yet, it is said to alleviate many of mental and emotional struggles – from anxiety and depression, to excessive overthinking. In fact, in various Asian civilizations, people have been meditating for thousands of years. Surely, there must be something to it, then!

Furthermore, the curious simplicity of meditation can be unnerving in a society riddled with products and hacks and noise. What do you mean you just sit there and do nothing? What do you watch? What do you listen to? What do I need to buy? Nothing. Yes, this can be enlightening in itself this day and age.

But I argue that as life gets busier, then meditation only becomes more profound. The more we do, the more special it is to do nothing.

So don't overthink meditation, at least! Don't waste time looking for elaborate techniques or methods. Just remember that "simple" doesn't necessarily mean "easy"... in fact, modern life has perhaps made "simple" the hardest thing of all for us to grasp. As such, meditation is both the ultimate challenge and the ultimate relief. As put by executive coach and pro-meditator Ravi Raman, 'its simplicity is a disguise.'

And so, meditation can be used as a way to reconnect with yourself and become more attuned to your bodily sensations and senses. It can be a great way to encourage your mind to temporarily slow down to stop its constant thinking for a brief moment that can, with repeated practice, improve your overthinking habit even when you're not engaging in the practice. It is essentially a way to close all the open tabs of your mind, as you would your computer (most of us have far too many in both contexts!). To reboot it. Don't lose sight of the fact that your mind is under constant strain, and overthinking is only further burdening it, making it more likely to crash or over-heat.

# Meditation and mindfulness
*How can meditation work for you?*

And here's that word again: mindfulness.
It may sound contradictory to suggest incorporating something called "mindfulness" in order to make your mind less...well...full. However, mindfulness is all about allowing thoughts to come and go - acknowledging and being aware of every thought and emotion, yet not letting any of them stick around and sour into rumination. It's about, as touched upon previously, living in the moment. Feeling the oxygen flood your body with every breath, the breeze on your face, the warmth of your toes in your socks, and the faint chirping of birds in the distance. It's about sharpening your senses and yet not letting any of them overwhelm you.
The thing is, the modern way of life is full of contradictions. Just as we overstimulate our senses with screens and headphones and overthinking, we somehow also manage to become somewhat senorily numb when it comes to more organic stimulation - such as the triggers mentioned above. As such, our minds become cluttered with he-said-that's, and notifications, and emails, and advertisements - and yet leave no room for the more wholesome

stimuli of nature, meaningful face-to-face conversations, and smiles from strangers. Is it any wonder our brains are frazzled with stimulation, and yet we still keep craving more?

Not only is mindfulness about learning to live in the present and stop constant mental "time travel," but it is an entire way of living and of being. Whether you adopt daily meditation, yoga, or tai chi ritual - or prefer a quiet walk on your lunch break - your overburdened brain is desperate for this moment to pause and detach from otherwise constant mental stimuli. It's about giving your mind the space to wander and simply paying attention to what you're sensing without any particular agenda, purpose or self-criticism.

Mindfulness is relevant both when you are meditating and when you are not. Of course, a big part of meditation is allowing your mind to reconnect with the present in this way, and to loosen your grip on the worries and intrusive thoughts that threaten your peace. However, you can also work on being more mindful all the time - when you're working, interacting with others when you're going through a good time, or a more challenging time. Mindfulness is both a key component to the practice of meditation as well as a way of life. Although, like meditation, its roots are in eastern philosophy, it bears similarities to the western ideology of stoicism.

This Ancient Greek school of thought pioneered by philosophers such as Seneca and Epictetus can still offer a fresh perspective on freeing ourselves from overthinking and living a more mindful life to this day. For instance, as put by Epictetus:

'When someone is properly grounded in life, they shouldn't have to look outside themselves for approval.'

Similarly, Seneca famously said:

'True happiness is to enjoy the present, without anxious dependence upon the future, not to amuse ourselves with either hopes or fears but to rest satisfied with what we have, which is sufficient, for he that is so, wants nothing.'

## How To Meditate

Bearing all of this wisdom - ancient and modern; eastern and western - in mind, also note that the most successful way to meditate is to do so without too much expectation, and certainly without self-criticism. In truth, it doesn't actually matter how you're sitting, or whether or not you play music, or have the light on. You could do it lying down, in bed, in the bath, or at your desk. Whenever you get an opportunity to switch off for a few short moments, in order to give your mind that valuable reboot that it so craves, and continue your day with a newfound sense of mental clarity and purpose.

Don't fret if rogue thoughts enter your head, either. You haven't failed. Don't just throw in the towel or claim meditation to be stupid because you don't quite get it the first couple of attempts. The more you overthink about having a clear mind, or getting things done "how they are supposed to be," the more your rumination threatens your inner peace.

Simply allow your thought processes to flow organically, perhaps gently ushering them towards a key mantra or focus that you selected for your practice- for instance "I am exactly where I need to be," or "I will not worry about what I cannot control." Will all other chatter in the back of your mind to at least quieten into a soft hum. And then, just wait and see where your mind takes you once it is freed from its usual shackles of obsessive, compulsive thoughts.

# Find your ideal meditation
*Pranayama: Nadi Shodhana and Brahmari*

I propose that the best meditation exercises, especially if you suffer from anxiety as a result of your overthinking, is 'Pranayama,' - which literally means 'control of breath.' I highly recommend, as a first step to using your physical body to calm your mind,
you start being more conscious of your breathing. At first, it may seem strange, but then you will realize that thinking about your breath is working diverting your thoughts from your worries.

The word "prana" alone means vital energy. According to ancient Hindu beliefs, this spiritual spark or energy source and the mind are intimately connected (and today, this is somewhat backed up from what scientists have discussed about the brain's electromagnetic waves!). In terms of this apparent duality between "prana" and the physical mind, the idea behind Pranayama meditation states that controlling one helps to balance out the other. However, when there is an imbalance between the two, both physical and mental complications can arise. Indeed, chronic overthinking is often a result of this imbalance between the mind and "prana." Bringing harmony between the "prana" and the mind is the aim of Pranayama meditation.

**Pranayama Breathing Exercises for Overthinking**

Okay, if all this talk of "prana" and spiritualism is a little far-fetched for your tastes, let's get to the science. Did you know that slowing down your breathing actually raises the carbon dioxide level in the blood? But this isn't as scary as it sounds. It is actually necessary for relaxation - for instance, while you are sleeping. This is because it tips its pH level back to a slightly more acidic and less alkaline state. As such,
the blood's pH decreases, and the nervous system naturally calms you down.

Your breath can be a hugely powerful ally when it comes to building the resilience to cope with temporary states of either mental, physical, or emotional strain—whether you're grappling with anger after being wronged by a loved one, having a stressful day at work, or are anxiously ruminating about a particular responsibility. A clearer mind will help any given situation - no matter how anxiety-ridden you may feel in the moment. Taking the time to control your breath can be truly life-changing.

It may feel strange and unnatural at first to be actively conscious of your own breathing. Breathing is an instinct, after all. We are born knowing how to do it. As such, it has become so habitual that it feels rather odd to give it much attention. However, although instinctual to breathe, the way in which you breathe is under your control - and is perhaps one of the most untapped tools when it comes to taking care of our bodies and minds.

You'll probably find that once you pay attention to your breathing, you are breathing much shallower and faster than would be best. Most of the time, we don't make use of the vast space in our lungs, and capacity for all that oxygenated air we are completely dependent on to survive. Considering oxygen is fundamental to our survival and is - for the most part - in abundant supply -we can be rather stingy with ourselves!

Breathe deeply. Let your chest become filled with the air at your disposal. Feel your body drink in the oxygen and let it dissipate throughout your system. You are alive. You have air to breathe. This is literally your number one priority. So allow yourself to just fill your mind with this thought alone - the same way you are filling your lungs.

Is that better?

There is so much more to meditative breathing exercises than that. Here are a few ancient Indian breathing exercises that you can try your hand at next time your overthinking is beginning to creep up again:

**Nadi Shodhana Breathing**

Nadi Shodhana breathing is intended to purify the mind and body while supplying the body with additional oxygen. This helps to sharpen concentration, and yet slows down thought-processes to a manageable level.

To give it a try, simply sit in an upright position. Form a fist in your right hand but leave the thumb, ring finger, and little finger sticking out. Then press the right thumb onto the right side of the nose to cut off the air supply from one nostril. Inhale deeply. Hold it. And finally, release the thumb and press the ring finger of that same hand onto the left nostril. Repeat the practice on this side, then continue alternating nostrils between three and ten times. You will finish feeling a lot calmer, and your mind a lot clearer.

## Ujjayi Pranayama Breathing

Ujjayi Pranayama breathing, also known as the "ocean breath" practice, calms down the overthinking mind by soothing your nervous system. It has been proven to relieve insomnia and overthinking.

For this one, sit in an upright position again, this time lightly constricting the glottis (in your throat) so that you can hear a faint "snoring" sound as you breathe - this will help to slow it down. Inhale deeply through the nose, so that you are completely filling your lungs. Next, exhale completely, also through the nose. Repeat for as long as you need to - until your heart rate slows, calm begins to wash over you, and those obsessive or intrusive thoughts start to drift away with your breath.

## Kapalbhati Breathing

Now for a slightly more advanced pranayama breathing exercise: Kapalbhati breathing is said to cleanse the mind, body, and spirit. Essentially, it works by sending more oxygen to the brain, allowing it to function more effectively, while also balancing the nervous system, and strengthening the digestive system.

You guessed it: start by sitting in an upright position; Rest your hands on your knees or lower abdomen and then inhale deeply through the nose. Next, contract your lower abdominal muscles, and release the breath in short bursts. After one minute has passed, most likely having completely emptied your lungs in around 65-70 short exhalation bursts, inhale deeply through the nose again, and then exhale slowly fully through the mouth. Then inhale deeply again and repeat these quick exhalations, gradually increasing the exhalation bursts per minute, if it feels comfortable to do so. Repeat only two or three times and see how you feel after.

## Ajapa Japa Meditation

Ajapa Japa meditation is unique in its combination of meditation, pranayama breathing, and the final ingredient: mantra chanting. Mindfulness is also a big part of this one. "Ajapa Japa" literally translates as 'the awareness and experience of a mantra' in Sanskrit. You simply repeat a mantra of your choice. Make it something meaningful and personal to you - such as 'I will not worry about what I cannot change,' 'I am strong and can achieve whatever I want,' or 'everything I need is within me.'

Eventually, after many repeats, the mantra is said to "come to life" and forms part of your consciousness. By this stage, you no longer even need to actively repeat the mantra, because it has become so ingrained into your subconscious that you are now immersed in it - and hopefully, this seeps into your behaviors and thinking patterns! This level of meditation mastery can take anything from a few months, right up to several years, for the real pros. It may seem like a long game, but even when first starting this unique ancient practice, you start to feel the benefit. It should not be regarded as a chore, but a joy - a nourishing activity for your mind, and an opportunity for active, positive, self-talk that can actually shape how you see yourself and how you think through challenging situations. It is said to increase self-awareness, mental clarity, and encourage positive thinking and mindfulness.

But for this to work, you must practice detachment. Observe your thoughts, even the negative ones, but don't let them consume you.

Don't wallow in the past or fear the future. Just allow yourself to be in the moment and focus on the one key message you would like to manifest through your mantra.

### Brahmari Breathing

Brahmari breathing focuses on the tight-chested feeling that many anxious overthinkers are all-too-familiar with. This ancient practice is designed to calm the mind and open up the lungs at the same time, leaving your mind grounded, and your thoughts slowed. To practice Brahmari Pranayama, sit comfortably, with your spine straight, and your shoulders relaxed. Then close your eyes and take a few regular breaths - not forcing them to be neither deep or shallow, but just going with your natural rhythm. Then, take one deep breath through the nose to fill your lungs to full capacity. While you slowly exhale, make a humming sound. Hold this sound until you empty your lung cavity and need to inhale again. Then inhale through the nose again and repeat, humming through your exhalation. Continue by inhaling naturally and then exhaling with this sound for several minutes. Practice this exercise for as long as you need to feel your optimum level of calm.

The longer you continue the hum, the more of a relaxing effect it is likely to have. However, note that pushing the limits of your natural lung capacity too far can only lead to even more stress. So don't force anything - this is supposed to be relaxing, not a strain!

## How Meditation Helps Brain Function

Although much research has been done over the last few decades, the precise effects of meditation on our electroencephalographic (EEG) brain activity are still in the process of being defined.

There has been a huge surge in scientific studies on meditation in the last ten years. This piqued interest in such an ancient practice in the age of technology that allows for detailed brain imaging means that we can now approach meditation in a completely new light. These studies have demonstrated time and time again the various beneficial effects of meditative practices on one's perception, mental cognition, emotional processing, and even neuroplasticity (the ability for your brain to adapt and form new neural connections).

For instance, a recent analysis on neuroimaging studies over around 300 meditation practitioners revealed that practicing meditation is consistently associated with an adapted morphology of the prefrontal cortex and body awareness regions.

Although we are only just seeing the tip of the iceberg when it comes to the effect of meditation on the brain, due to the limitations of EEG imaging (this can only measure brain activity in real-time - and it's not easy to meditate in a cold doctor's office with probes attached to your head, being watched intently!) expert meditators have been shown to experience an increase in their Gamma waves, which suggests they are more able to reach an inner state of calm even when not meditating. These Gamma waves were initially dismissed as 'spare brain noise' when detected on the first EEG imaging tests - that's until it was discovered that these waves are highly active when the subject is in states of love, altruism, or so-called 'higher virtues'. So what could this mean? Whether or not you choose to read into it as evidence of spirituality or a higher power, one thing we can agree in is that a special type of brain activity can be reached only when we are filled with positivity, and literal "good vibes."

Gamma waves are also above the frequency of neuronal firing, so precisely how they are generated remains a mystery! They are the fastest, highest-frequency of brain waves and allow the simultaneous processing of information from different brain areas, passing information both rapidly and effortlessly. Could this relate to the flow state discussed earlier? When the brain is both in peak productivity and peak relaxation? The jury is still out when it comes to exactly what all of this means. But when it comes to how it affects your overthinking and meditation habit, just know that as the most "subtle" of the brainwave frequencies, the mind has to be at peace, to access them. As such, it's crucial to find the best time, emotionally balanced state, and the perfect frequency for successful, gamma-sparking meditation.

## The Bottom Line: Fix your body, fix your mind

As we have now seen, mindfulness and meditation can be life-changing for those with over-active, over-analytical minds getting in the way of how they live their life. If up until now, you have been skeptical of meditation and its tangible benefits, or simply have tried and haven't had much luck in the past, with a little patience and an open mind, you can allow it to take you to a new realm of self-awareness and become an observer of your own thoughts in the true stoic sense.

Surely it speaks for itself that both eastern and western philosophies share this common threat of letting go of your thoughts, emotions, and distractions in order to find true peace and maintain mental clarity. Now that these ideologies are just entering the mainstream once again, as the pendulum is starting to swing back the other way after decades - or arguably, centuries - of consuming, performing, and thinking non-stop - the recent surge in popularity ma make it seem like a fad, but it is more of a renaissance! Is it any wonder, looking at how modern life has us more mentally stimulated, and yet emotionally disconnected than ever, that we are collectively craving a space to do and think nothing. Your body and mind are craving it, so listen!

Whether it's one of the breathing exercises detailed earlier, sitting still and allowing your thoughts to quieten, or simply striving to become more mindful and slow down in your day-to-day life - try to somehow slow down and reconnect with your mind. Give it the break and nourishment that it deserves.

# Conclusions

To wrap up, let's go over the key messages that you can walk away with after putting down this book. What can you take away from this journey? How can you implement through the rest of your life, and become a little better at handling your thought patterns? How can you implement the techniques and messages you've learned into your own day-to-day life?

## What have we learned about overthinking and anxiety?

I encourage you to take away the following key points on overthinking, armored with the knowledge you need to overcome this common habit, and become more present and fulfilled in your life.

First of all, although it may seem like you are the only one facing that tall unsurmountable wall of racing or intrusive thoughts when you start to spiral into an episode of rumination, rest assured that you are not alone. Almost everyone has faced a very similar inner turmoil at some point - many people go through it on the regular! But just as overthinking isn't a disorder or cause for major alarm, neither is it the best way for our minds to operate. However, in order to achieve maximum productivity as well as maximum emotional wellbeing - we need a healthy, clear, and balanced state of mind.

Furthermore, you must focus on your present by forgiving the past, learning from mistakes, and practice self-forgiveness. Accept that you simply can't predict the future - as much as you may try! A better use of your time and mental energy would be to overcome your fear of failure and manage the pressure you put on yourself, thanks to social expectations.

As you will recall, a key part of being at peace with yourself is trusting your instincts. Of course, that doesn't mean believing that you are invincible, or that you can do no wrong. A degree of thinking and strategy is always required. But aim to let go of obsessive, niggling negativity that threatens to hold you back or deter you from reaching your goals, whatever they are. Or an irrational quest for perfection that means you will never feel ready or good enough – when you often already are!

To help you achieve this, you can try tapping into your flow state – that perfect balance between rest and stimulation in order to perform and feel your best whatever you do. Then, get rid of mental junk by practicing mental minimalism and decluttering your mind. Organize your mind at work by planning – but also including sufficient breaks within this plan. Recognize that taking breaks – just like eating, drinking and sleeping – are all a part of your success and mental clarity.

Just as you shouldn't overthink at work, don't overthink your relationships – and don't forget those telling studies I shared with you! The more you analyze your relationship, the more "problems" you will identify. We all have real problems, sure – but avoid thinking further problems into existence – that's the last thing any of us need!

Remember that you are not defined by your thoughts, but more so what you actually do. As such, it's key to change your habits. Incorporate an optimal daily routine for both your mental and physical health.

Change your environment when necessary. This means giving your mind a break by changing the scenery – whether that's working on something new for a while, taking a walk, or taking a shower! A quick and simple break from whatever it is that's setting your mind in a spin can be a humble yet transformative way to boost your brainpower while giving your mind a break from frantic overthinking.

Don't forget to strive for excellence instead of perfection. Try to be a "perfect imperfectionist" instead– by being productive but in a

more healthy and balanced way, and stop chasing the unreachable and anxiety-fueling myth of perfection!

Fight chronic indecisiveness and decision fatigue by not sweating the small stuff and making room for the bigger issues in your life. You will now be able to implement the 40/70 rule of decision-making to avoid either diving in completely unprepared, or, on the opposite side of the spectrum, being too afraid to take any action unless you know every single detail - often meaning you either never take the action you need to, or only feel "prepared" when that ship has sailed....

You now also know the main causes of procrastination and why do you really put off the work you know you need to do - whether it's from a place of fear of failing, simply not giving yourself the mental energy required, or overthinking every detail to the point that you are too overwhelmed to begin... I hope you have now identified your own main obstacles, and how to get around these to stop procrastination from holding you back. Overall, you will recognize any self-sabotaging behaviors from now on: where they come from, and how to stop them in their tracks.

Finally, I am happy to have equipped you with the basic theories behind mindfulness and meditation, and how these ideologies can enable you to live more in the present, and feel both more self-motivated and calmer. You will now be pretty darn knowledgeable when it comes to how fixing your body is key to fixing your mind - as you cannot have one flourish without the other, as well as how to utilize the power of breathing and rest for mental clarity. Not to forget your now-thorough knowledge of the basics of pranayama breathing exercises - from your Nadi Shodhana to your Brahmari...

Okay, it may take some re-reading of that part for it all to sink in! But just think how cultured you will seem to bring up these terms at your next party... (You're very welcome!)

Stop Overthinking! Some Final Thoughts

It's true that we all naturally feel good when we have success, or feel validated by others. This drive to succeed, just as our tendency to think deeply, are not inherently unhealthy habits to keep. However, if you place too much of your worth or even identity down to this constantly just-out-of-reach idea of perfection, and dream of success that is always one more achievement away, we will never truly have inner-peace or calm the storm in your mind.

You must learn to feel fulfilled and worthy no matter what comes your way, and regardless of what you achieve. This is truly the most powerful way to lay your overthinking habit to rest - to simply be - and be content in doing so! To understand that you are not perfect - because you are human. And to realize that making mistakes should not sentence you to a lifetime of ruminating over what went wrong, or berating yourself constantly in your mind, needlessly re-living any negative emotions you experienced...

Okay, I admit, it's easier said than done to break these habits of a lifetime that take root way back into childhood. That being said, you must start giving our own opinions the respect and consideration that they deserve, and learning to make peace both with your past and all the possible scenarios of the future, in order to focus on the present to live a fulfilled and mindful life.

So take a moment to reflect on what you truly want each day. No, not tomorrow - but right now. What do you need? The chances are, what you really need is a lot less than you think once you take away the worries of tomorrow. Imagine living most of your days in such a carefree manner, far away from any intrusive worries about what tomorrow may bring?

So next time your thoughts start to race, and you start to obsess about something irrationally, convincing yourself that the worst-case-scenario will happen, just remember where you're at right now: The oxygen entering your body; the absence of an immediate threat to your life. You are okay. And whatever is threatening your peace - most likely - can wait. Your own emotional wellbeing should not only take priority, but it is the key to your mental capacity anyway. Only when you are mentally sound can you have any hope of solving your problems anyway! So remember that next time your anxiety levels rise, and you lose all hope.

Your negative thoughts only matter as much as you let them. And although it sometimes doesn't feel like it, you have some level of control over your own peace of thoughts and the emotions that they inspire - and this control can be worked on with patience and practice. And once you open your eyes to your potential to manipulate what you let affect you mentally, you will experience true emotional resilience.

## The Bottom Line

I initially promised you that if you manage to let go of damaging thoughts and mental habits, that your mind would feel lighter, clearer, and more resilient to tackle any real problems you have - with all the unnecessary worries no longer cluttering your precious mental space and draining your precious mental energy.

By now, I trust you have a deep understanding of what overthinking truly is - how it can be harmful and counterproductive - and perhaps most importantly, how you can overcome it and keep your mind a much clearer and healthier place to be. I trust you will now feel more driven, with a clearer direction in mind - both in terms of your success in life, but also in terms of how to improve your relationship with your own mind, and how to reconnect with yourself to stop being a slave to your anxiety, unconscious worries and intrusive thoughts.

To finish with a quote by the 14th century Persian Poet, Hafez, that I hope will allow you to walk away today with the right mindset:

"Now that your worry has proved such an unlucrative business, Why not find a better job?"

*Sebastian O'Brien*

# References

4 Reasons to Stop Worrying About the Future. (2012, July 26). Retrieved May 20, 2020, from https://www.embracethechaos.com/2012/07/4-reasons-to-stop-worrying-about-the-future/

6 Tips for Overcoming Anxiety-Related Procrastination. (2013). Retrieved June 10, 2020, from https://www.psychologytoday.com/us/blog/in-practice/201303/6-tips-overcoming-anxiety-related-procrastination

8 Ways to Stop Self-Sabotaging Your Success. (2018). Retrieved June 10, 2020, from https://www.entrepreneur.com/article/324900

Aldrey, M. (2019, June 8). Leverage Your Unique Energy Levels for Maximum Productivity. Retrieved May 21, 2020, from https://groovywink.com/energy-maximum-productivity/

Assari, S. (2016, June 22). Why stress is more likely to cause depression in men than in women. Retrieved from https://theconversation.com/why-stress-is-more-likely-to-cause-depression-in-men-than-in-women-57624

Azimy, R. (2020a, January 10). Somatic Experiencing: Restoring Balance to Heal Trauma. Retrieved from https://www.selfishdarling.com/2019/12/28/somatic-experiencing-restoring-balance-to-heal-trauma/

Azimy, R. (2020b, January 11). Alternatives to meditation for chatty minds. Retrieved June 17, 2020, from https://www.selfishdarling.com/inspiration/alternatives-to-meditation-for-chatty-minds/

Azimy, R. (2020c, April 3). The Secret to Contentment? Treat Your Emotions like the Weather. Retrieved May 18, 2020, from https://medium.com/illumination/the-secret-to-contentment-treat-yor-emotions-like-the-weather-bc7a51fc9e1a

Azimy, R. (2020d, April 27). So You Want to be More "ZEN"? - ILLUMINATION. Retrieved June 17, 2020, from https://medium.com/illumination/so-you-want-to-be-more-zen-65def826ab09?source=---------16------------------

Azimy, R. (2020e, May 4). Deepak Chopra's Meditation Challenge: 6 Lessons I Learned. Retrieved May 18, 2020, from https://www.selfishdarling.com/holistic-healing/deepak-chopras-meditation-challenge-6-lessons-i-learned/

Baer, D. (2015, April 28). The scientific reason why Barack Obama and Mark Zuckerberg wear the same outfit every day. Retrieved June 4, 2020, from https://www.businessinsider.com/barack-obama-mark-zuckerberg-wear-the-same-outfit-2015-4?r=US&IR=T

Boogaard, K. (2020, May 11). The Little-Known Reason You're So Indecisive. Retrieved June 4, 2020, from https://www.themuse.com/advice/the-littleknown-reason-youre-so-indecisive

Boyes, A. (2018, May 16). How to Stop Sabotaging Yourself. Retrieved June 10, 2020, from https://greatergood.berkeley.edu/article/item/how_to_stop_sabotaging_yourself

Cameron, K. S., & Spreitzer, G. M. (2012). *The Oxford Handbook of Positive Organizational Scholarship*. Oxford, United Kingdom: Oxford University Press.

Cannon, J. (2016, July 13). We All Want to Fit In. Retrieved May 27, 2020, from https://www.psychologytoday.com/us/blog/brainstorm/201607/we-all-want-fit-in

D. (2020a, January 6). 4 Types of Procrastination and How to Beat Them. Retrieved June 10, 2020, from https://alphaefficiency.com/4-types-procrastination-beat/

Daskal, L. (2020a, February 6). 10 Simple Ways You Can Stop Yourself From Overthinking. Retrieved May 20, 2020, from https://www.inc.com/lolly-daskal/10-simple-ways-you-can-stop-yourself-from-overthinking.html

Daskal, L. (2020b, February 6). 10 Simple Ways You Can Stop Yourself From Overthinking. Retrieved July 1, 2020, from https://www.inc.com/lolly-daskal/10-simple-ways-you-can-stop-yourself-from-overthinking.html

Day, S. (n.d.). Stress Nutrition Advice - Nutritionist Resource. Retrieved June 11, 2020, from https://www.nutritionist-resource.org.uk/articles/stress.html#stressanddiet

Dean, C. (2019, July 1). What Is Mental Minimalism. Retrieved May 20, 2020, from https://www.clarissadean.com/blog/mental-minimalism

deloitteeditor. (2017, May 12). How Stress Affects Team Dynamics. Retrieved May 14, 2020, from https://deloitte.wsj.com/cmo/2017/01/19/how-stress-affects-team-dynamics/

Developing a Mental Framework for Effective Thinking. (2020, January 3). Retrieved May 20, 2020, from https://fs.blog/2015/03/mental-framework/

Dollard, Maureen F, Dormann, C., Tuckey, M. R., & Escartín, J. (2017). Psychosocial safety climate (PSC) and enacted PSC for workplace bullying and psychological health problem reduction. *European Journal of Work and Organizational Psychology*, 26(6), 844–857. https://doi.org/10.1080/1359432x.2017.1380626

Dollard, M.F., Dormann, C., & Idris, A. M. (2019). *Psychosocial Safety Climate: A New Work Stress Theory* (1st ed. 2019 ed.). Heidelberg, Denmark: Springer.

Dunne, C. (2019, June 6). The Power of Single-Tasking. Retrieved May 21, 2020, from https://www.tameday.com/the-power-of-single-tasking/

Edberg, H. (2020, May 14). How to Stop Overthinking Everything: 12 Simple Habits. Retrieved June 18, 2020, from https://www.positivityblog.com/how-to-stop-overthinking/

Editor, HRreview. (2019, August 9). It costs over £30K to replace a staff member. Retrieved May 19, 2020, from https://www.hrreview.co.uk/hr-news/recruitment/it-costs-over-30k-to-replace-a-staff-member/50677

Everything you NEED to Know About The 40/70 Rule! (n.d.). Retrieved June 4, 2020, from https://marketingreleased.com/everything-you-need-to-know-about-the-4070-rule/

Fader, S. (2017, June 2). What Is Overthinking Disorder? | BetterHelp. Retrieved from https://www.betterhelp.com/advice/personality-disorders/what-is-overthinking-disorder/

Fahkry, T. (2018, June 20). Here's Why You Are Not Your Thoughts. Retrieved May 21, 2020, from https://medium.com/the-mission/heres-why-you-are-not-your-thoughts-5459b0b96ba0

Fields, K. (2017, May 15). The Imperfection of Perfectionism. Retrieved May 27, 2020, from https://www.talkspace.com/blog/the-imperfection-of-perfectionism/

Fletcher, B. (2019, June 20). Struggling to sleep? How to avoid overthinking when you get in to bed. Retrieved May 21, 2020, from https://www.netdoctor.co.uk/healthy-living/a28687/overthinking-cant-sleep/

How Perfectionism Can Contribute to Anxiety. (2020, March 22). Retrieved May 27, 2020, from https://www.verywellmind.com/perfectionism-and-panic-disorder-2584391#

How to Cure the Perfectionist Habit. (2013, December 2). Retrieved May 27, 2020, from https://gatorworks.net/how-to-cure-the-perfectionist-habit/

How to support mental health at work. (2020, April 30). Retrieved May 26, 2020, from https://www.mentalhealth.org.uk/publications/how-support-mental-health-work

Huffington, A. (2014a). *Thrive*. Zaltbommel, Netherlands: Van Haren Publishing.

Huffington, A. (2014b). *Thrive*. Zaltbommel, Netherlands: Van Haren Publishing.

Increased Gamma Brainwave Amplitude Compared to Control in Three Different Meditation Traditions. (2017, January 24). Retrieved June 17, 2020, from https://www.ncbi.nlm.nih.gov/pmc/articles/PMC5261734/

Insights Discovery part 1: The 4 colors. (2018). Retrieved June 12, 2020, from https://www.mudamasters.com/en/personal-growth-personality/insights-discovery-part-1-4-colors

Jones, M. (2018, September 11). 5 Ways Minimalism Is Good For Your Mental Health. Retrieved May 20, 2020, from https://www.aconsciousrethink.com/6881/minimalism-mental-health/

Jordan, R. (2019, July 26). How to Stop Overthinking. Retrieved June 17, 2020, from https://www.yogi.press/home/how-to-stop-overthinking

Kahn, W. A. (1990). Psychological Conditions of Personal Engagement and Disengagement at Work. *Academy of Management Journal*, 33(4), 692–724. https://doi.org/10.5465/256287

Kumar, M. (2009, December 7). Difference Between Reflection and Introspection. Retrieved from http://www.differencebetween.net/miscellaneous/difference-between-reflection-and-introspection/

Markway, B. (2013, January 14). Pursuing Excellence, Not Perfection. Retrieved May 26, 2020, from https://www.psychologytoday.com/us/blog/shyness-is-nice/201301/pursuing-excellence-not-perfection+

Maros, M. (2016, October 31). How to Deal with Indecision. Retrieved June 4, 2020, from https://peacefulmindpeacefullife.org/how-to-deal-with-indecision/

Morin, A. (2019a, January 19). 10 Signs You're an Overthinker. Retrieved June 22, 2020, from https://thriveglobal.com/stories/signs-you-overthink-things/

Morin, A. (2019b, October 15). The Difference Between Helpful Problem Solving And Harmful Overthinking. Retrieved from https://www.forbes.com/sites/amymorin/2019/10/15/the-difference-between-helpful-problem-solving-and-harmful-overthinking/#3dc86c156e5f

Nwatarali, G. (2018, May 5). 5 Tips To Overcome Laziness And Procrastination. Retrieved June 10, 2020, from https://lifestylebusinessmag.com/5-tips-overcome-laziness-procrastination/

Oracles, T. (2019, June 25). 11 Genius Tips to Be More Decisive. Retrieved June 4, 2020, from https://www.success.com/11-genius-tips-to-be-more-decisive/

Oshin, M. (2019, May 23). Elon Musks' "3-Step" First Principles Thinking: How to Think and Solve Difficult Problems Like a.... Retrieved May 20, 2020, from https://medium.com/the-mission/elon-musks-3-step-first-principles-thinking-how-to-think-and-solve-difficult-problems-like-a-ba1e73a9f6c0

Perfection and Anxiety:How Perfection Can Increase Anxiety. (n.d.). Retrieved May 26, 2020, from https://discoverymood.com/blog/perfectionism-can-increase-anxiety/

Peterson, C., & Seligman, M. (2004). *Character Strengths and Virtues: A Handbook and Classification* (1st ed.). Oxford, United Kingdom: American Psychological Association / Oxford University Press.

Peterson, Christopher, & Park, N. (2006). Character strengths in organizations. *Journal of Organizational Behavior, 27*(8), 1149–1154. https://doi.org/10.1002/job.398

Petticrew, M. P., Lee, K., & McKee, M. (2012). Type A Behavior Pattern and Coronary Heart Disease: Philip Morris's "Crown Jewel." *American Journal of Public Health, 102*(11), 2018–2025. https://doi.org/10.2105/ajph.2012.300816

Pfeffer, J. (2018, May 3). How your workplace is killing you. Retrieved June 19, 2020, from https://www.bbc.com/worklife/article/20180502-how-your-workplace-is-killing-you

Porath, C., Spreitzer, G., Gibson, C., & Garnett, F. G. (2011). Thriving at work: Toward its measurement, construct validation, and theoretical refinement. *Journal of Organizational Behavior, 33*(2), 250–275. https://doi.org/10.1002/job.756

Qureshi, H. (2018, January 29). Being in the zone: A matter of extreme focus. Retrieved May 20, 2020, from https://medium.com/@HassanQureshi/being-in-the-zone-a-matter-of-extreme-focus-7d37585c75b4

Raman, R. (2018, June 21). 11 Simple Ways To Stop Overthinking Everything And Take Control Of Your Life. Retrieved May 21, 2020, from https://medium.com/the-mission/11-simple-ways-to-stop-overthinking-everything-and-take-control-of-your-life-cf6de0b8d83f

Ravi Raman. (2018, February 22). Meditation is the Ultimate Life Hack You Aren't Using. Retrieved June 17, 2020, from https://raviraman.com/meditation-life-hack/

Rosen, R. (2007, August 28). Pranayama Practices for Stress, Anxiety, and Depression. Retrieved June 17, 2020, from https://www.yogajournal.com/yoga-101/inhale-exhale-relax-and-energize

Ruggeri, A. (2018). The dangerous downsides of perfectionism. Retrieved May 26, 2020, from https://www.bbc.com/future/article/20180219-toxic-perfectionism-is-on-the-rise

Self-Sabotage: Overcoming Self-Defeating Behavior. (n.d.). Retrieved June 10, 2020, from https://www.mindtools.com/pages/article/newTCS_95.htm

Sinicki, A. (2017, January 7). The Philosophy of Bruce Lee - On Flow, Self-Actualization, Creativity, Willpower and More. Retrieved May 20, 2020, from https://www.thebioneer.com/philosophy-bruce-lee-flow-self-actualization-creativity-willpower/

Stress Puts Double Whammy On Reproductive System, Fertility. (2009). Retrieved May 14, 2020, from https://www.sciencedaily.com/releases/2009/06/090615171618.htm

Symptoms That Mimic Epilepsy LInked to Stress, Poor Coping Skills - 04/10/2012. (2012). Retrieved May 18, 2020, from https://www.hopkinsmedicine.org/news/media/releases/symptoms_that_mimic_epilepsy_linked_to_stress_poor_coping_skills

Systolic Blood Pressure Intervention Trial (SPRINT) Study | National Heart, Lung, and Blood Institute (NHLBI). (2018, July 25). Retrieved June 12, 2020, from https://www.nhlbi.nih.gov/science/systolic-blood-pressure-intervention-trial-sprint-study

Teeth grinding (bruxism). (2020, May 11). Retrieved May 25, 2020, from https://www.nhs.uk/conditions/teeth-grinding/

The future of future-oriented cognition in non-humans: theory and the empirical case of the great apes. (2014, November 5). Retrieved May 18, 2020, from https://www.ncbi.nlm.nih.gov/pmc/articles/PMC4186238/

the Healthline Editorial Team. (2017, September 28). 5 Steps for Overcoming Indecision. Retrieved June 4, 2020, from https://www.healthline.com/health/5-steps-overcoming-indecision

Thibodeaux, W. (2020, February 6). The 3 Main Types of Procrastinators, According to Psychology. Retrieved June 10, 2020, from https://www.inc.com/wanda-thibodeaux/the-3-main-types-of-procrastinators-according-to-psychology.html

Trapani, G. (2012, August 4). Work Smart: Do Your Worst Task First (Or, Eat a Live Frog Every Morning). Retrieved May 21, 2020, from https://www.fastcompany.com/1592454/work-smart-do-your-worst-task-first-or-eat-live-frog-every-morning

(1970, January 19). How To Stop Overthinking Everything, According To Therapists. Retrieved from https://www.buzzfeed.com/ryanhowes/how-to-stop-ruminating

Weiss, S. (2017, December 11). 7 Reasons Why You're So Indecisive, According To Experts. Retrieved June 4, 2020, from https://www.bustle.com/p/7-reasons-why-youre-so-indecisive-according-to-experts-7427785

Y. (2019, November 28). The Different Types of Pranayama and When to Use Them. Retrieved June 17, 2020, from https://www.yogamatters.com/blog/different-types-of-pranayama-when-to-use-them/

Yeong, D. (2020). Why Tiny Actions Work Best, Way Better than Massive Action. Retrieved May 21, 2020, from https://deanyeong.com/tiny-actions-work-best/

Z. (2020b, May 11). Finding Flow: 5 Steps to Get in the Zone and Be More Productive. Retrieved May 20, 2020, from https://zapier.com/blog/how-to-find-flow/

Zimmer, C. (2007, April 2). Time in the Animal Mind. Retrieved May 18, 2020, from https://www.nytimes.com/2007/04/03/science/03time.html

Made in the USA
Las Vegas, NV
16 December 2021